"Christian life is a journey to transformation. The priesthood is not exempt from this painful process. With care and studied deliberation, Perri attempts to track how priesthood can move from trial to transformation. Readers cannot remain unmoved by this provocative analysis.

"No one can deny the radical challenge that the priesthood is undergoing in our times. We need wisdom and insight to understand how God's grace is at work in this crisis. William D. Perri brings to this task years of study and experience. His psychological analysis will disturb some, enlighten others. No one will be able to avoid pondering the essential questions. This book will create passionate dialogue."

✝ Robert F. Morneau
Chairman NCCB
Priestly Life and Ministry Committee

"William Perri's *A Radical Challenge for Priesthood Today* not only fleshes out the idea that 'by your wounds you are healed' but proclaims rather clearly that if there is to be a functional and living priesthood in the future, it will be built on present wounds. It is through the low morale among priests, religious, laity, and bishops; the fear of intimacy, depression, addiction, sexual difficulties, perfectionism, authoritarianism; and other painful disorders that priesthood is being transformed, by the very savage Grace of God."

John D. Powers, C.P.
Author, *Mirror, Mirror on the Wall*

"From years of practical experience Perri wisely challenges modern ministry and uses that same experience to broker understanding, healing, and renewal for priestly spirituality. This should be required reading for anyone interested in the priesthood."

A.W. Richard Sipe
Author, *Celibacy: A Way of Loving, Living, and Serving*

"What a breath of fresh air! William D. Perri's book is essential reading for anyone who is positively concerned with the Gospel message in today's world. What makes this book so appealing is the manner in which Perri addresses the challenge of priesthood today. It is easy to be negative, to point out all the deficiencies and disordered pathology. What we find here is the honest challenge of what priesthood can and should become in today's world, affirming the positive supports in tradition, spirituality, and healthy human living. My gratitude to William Perri for this needed contribution in such a positive light."

Very Rev. William J. Wiethorn, O.F.M. Cap.,
Definitor General

"William Perri has written an original, exhaustive, and challenging study on the priesthood today. He addresses the frightening spiritual, psychological, and social tornados that are now raging through the Catholic priesthood. His book is a call for innovative insights and radical responses—if priesthood is to be transformed. I found this book soul-nurturing, despite the complexity, diversity, and sheer weight of the problems confronting bishops and priests currently."

Very Rev. Liam J. Hoare, s.P.
Servant General

A RADICAL CHALLENGE FOR PRIESTHOOD TODAY

From Trial to Transformation

WILLIAM D. PERRI

TWENTY-THIRD PUBLICATIONS
Mystic, CT 06355

Dedication

To all those priests who,
by sharing their trials and brokenness,
have helped me to recognize the need for
transformation in the priesthood.

Second Printing 2002

Twenty-Third Publications
A Division of Bayard
185 Willow Street
P.O. Box 180
Mystic, CT 06355
(860) 536-2611
(800) 321-0411
www.twentythirdpublications.com

ISBN 0-89622-710-3
Library of Congress Catalog Card Number 96-60952
Printed in the U.S.A.

Contents

A RADICAL CHALLENGE FOR PRIESTHOOD TODAY

Introduction

The priesthood, as it exists in the West, as it has existed for many centuries of Catholic history, is struggling. It is gravely ill and breaking down. Some say it is in a nosedive, a state of collapse. Some argue it has already died and what the church is experiencing today is a painfully drawn-out funeral vigil. And if that is true, what comes next?[1]

Tom Fox's assessment is true, the priesthood as we know it is dying. We can see this in many areas, from the shortage of priests to the sexual and psychological problems that are so apparent now because of the media attention. Morale in the priesthood is extremely low. Many people fear that the priesthood will be lost forever in the midst of all these trials.

At the same time, we innately know that priesthood is an archetype that is necessary for the proper functioning of all people. It has a primary place in the preservation of the human race. So, we are confronted with a contradiction that is difficult to understand and can cause great fear. Priesthood appears throughout the history of this planet in many forms and roles. Modern, ordained priesthood is but one expression of a much larger pattern. Its ordained form can give us clues to the basic, underlying structure of priesthood in general and provide a model for understanding the inner dynamic of this archetypal organization, which is often unconscious. In searching for this paradigm we need to understand the various pathological disorders that appear in the lives of priests, because these are the signs of priesthood's death. The only way to rediscover the life of priesthood is to examine its decline and the reasons for it.

The disorders of priesthood can be serious problems. However, an acknowledgment of the pathological dynamics inherent in this vocation, along with endorsement of their grace-filled significance, can also be the beginning of a transformative process. A humble recognition and acceptance of these symptoms, such as sexual difficulties, depression, perfectionism, authoritarianism, and fear of intimacy, can become the source for a richer and more meaningful expression of priesthood's mediating role—and lead to a more vibrant manifestation of its meaning.

These reflections are the result of twenty years of experience working with priests in residential treatment programs, giving retreats and workshops to priests, doing spiritual direction and therapy with priests, and being a priest myself. Recently, much of my time has been spent in analyzing data from psychological testing instruments that priests have taken and in studying research that has been done over the past sixty years or so.

This book is written for all those who are interested in understanding and preserving the mediatory function of priesthood for the human race. It is not designed merely for those who are ordained or who hold a formal ministerial role in an institutionalized religion, even though they may be more immediately interested in this topic. Many people who are ordained may or may not have received the indelible mark of priesthood. For that matter, many who are not ordained may actually participate in this archetypal vocation. The function of priesthood is much broader than any institution or organization. Perhaps the priesthood has, for too long, held a special place. This is not to say that a certain exceptional nature is not a part of this vocation. In fact, it is. But priests have abused this distinctive gift by turning the priesthood into an exclusive and somewhat elitist hierarchy. Others who are not institutionally ordained have also experienced the true message of this vocation in their lives.

I believe that God is blessing the priesthood today with illness, psychological symptoms, and disheartening limitations in order to offer a clear message as to how it can be returned to its primordial intention. This is the fundamental reason why this book has been written: to suggest possibilities that can move the priesthood from trial to transformation. No one accepts death readily. And yet, with the eyes of faith we can believe that there is a great awakening on the other side of this death of priesthood: its reconstructed life! All of this darkness contains the light—we only need the eyes to see.

CHAPTER ONE

From Absence to Discovery

Sometimes God's absence helps.[1]

Several years ago a dream informed me. The only fragment of it that remained in my mind when I awoke was the Latin phrase *Deus absconditus*. As I searched for some significance to this phrase I was led to my dusty old Latin dictionary that has not been opened since my seminary days. *Abscondere* is a Latin verb meaning "to put away or to hide." As I further researched the roots of this word, I discovered that "to abscond," means "to be hidden away."[2] God is hidden away.

At the time that I experienced this dream, I was immersed in stacks of information concerning psychological disorders in the priesthood: books, articles, notes, and research documents. The message of this dream in some way seemed to be associated with this pile of papers. I was led to ask myself, "How can God be hidden away in this information?"

After pondering this question, it occurred to me that God is indeed overshadowing something here. My perspective, since I was writing a dissertation for my Ph.D. in clinical psychology, had been on statistics and numbers: how many priests have certain disorders, which symptoms are most interesting, which psychopathology is most common among priests, and how can I prove or disprove my hypotheses? The dream, however, seemed to suggest that another viewpoint can emerge from this information. The new task, then, in response to the dream, became: how to reveal the deeper, unconscious reality?

Contemporary theories interpret psychological disorders in the light of medical science: cures are sought; healing is the goal; order is the norm. For a change, let's take a contradictory perspective and follow the idea that God is hidden. What if the cure for these pathologies lies hidden in the very disorders themselves? What if, as in the view of the mystics, the darkness is the light? What if the pathologies of priesthood are themselves the revealer of God? God may very well be hidden in the illnesses. As Paul writes to the Corinthians, when he speaks of his thorn in the flesh which will not be healed or cured:

> God said to me: "My grace is enough for you, for in weakness, power reaches perfection" ... Therefore, I am content with weakness, ... for when I am powerless, it is then that I am strong (2 Corinthians 12: 9–10).

God is present in weakness and powerlessness, in chaos and disorder. A beautiful explanation of this is contained in Thomas Moore's book, *Care of the Soul*.[3]

God mysteriously hides in many ways. The Judeo-Christian Scriptures are filled with paradoxical and ambivalent passages that tell the tale of a God who is not always so apparent to the casual observer, and not always revealed as we might expect. God hides in suffering, in deficiency, in inadequacy, and in distress. In fact, Christian belief proclaims that the ultimate disorder, called death, is a most wonderful manifestation of God's new life. "For God's folly is wiser than people, and God's weakness is more powerful than people" (1 Corinthians 1:25).

How My Work Began

I first began my ministry to priests when I was a deacon. With another member of my religious congregation, I was assigned to a monastery in Albuquerque, New Mexico. When we arrived, two elderly priests were living in this house, but nothing was being done in terms of ministry. My friend and I were asked to begin some type of program to help priests. In reality, we had little idea of where to begin! Intuitively, however, we must have known that we could begin by looking at our own disorders. As we discussed our lives together, we both went into therapy to discern more clearly how our own pathological symptoms contained meaning. So, we began this ministry by sharing our own disorders and pain. Perhaps our problems could serve as an aid in helping other priests.

One of the first priests who came to this therapeutic program was suffering from some of the typical symptoms outlined in this book. He was depressed, lonely, extremely sensitive, unsure of his sexuality, but he was willing to pursue the depths of his own pain and darkness. He was an artist. He stayed in our struggling program for about seven months. When he was ready to leave, he presented us with the gift of a banner he had made. He said that it expressed the essence of his experience with us. The banner read: "Where you stumble and fall is where you find Gold." He explained that his own experience of darkness and pain had become the source of his ongoing healing and transformation. This banner became the motto for all the therapeutic programs that we would design and run for the next twenty years.

On the Way to Conversion

This book is about the transitions that priests experience as they stumble and fall through the midst of a serious conversion. Disorders emerge that have the potential to become either negative or positive, ignored or embraced. This is a solemn challenge for contemporary priesthood.

"Not in his goals but in his transitions man (sic) is great."[4] These words of Ralph Waldo Emerson describe the invitation facing the priesthood today. Transitions reveal the beginnings of an initiation rite from life to death and back again; they are a type of trance, a terrifying and inviting entrance. As a threshold, a transition can also be imagined as the archetypal *axis mundi*, or pole of the earth; it is the ladder of synchronized ascent and descent where angelic messengers go up and down (cf. Genesis 28:12–13).

A noted psychotherapist of this century, D.W. Winnicott, describes transitions as invitations for symbol making, times to "use fantasy, to call on inner reality and dream ..."[5] Priesthood, as mediation, is itself a transitional vocation, providing a linkage between one aspect of life and another. It offers an understanding of the mystery and ambivalence of life. Yet, if it cannot accept its own contradictions and undergo its own transformation, how can it possibly mediate them for others? And, because this is not happening, priesthood is dying. Transitional mediation lies at the very core of understanding the priestly vocation. Perhaps we need to listen more clearly to the meaning behind this truth.

The priesthood now has a prime opportunity to undergo its own metamorphosis. The low morale with which many people are concerned is a potential gift inviting priests to rediscover the hidden gold in this vocation. For this to happen, though, priests need to begin using their imaginations. I believe that God is trying to inspire the priesthood through all of the disorders that are no longer held in secret. The symbols of transformation for the priesthood are fashioned in the symptoms of depression, in perfectionism, in the abuses of power and authority, in role flexibility, in passivity, in aggression, and in contradiction. These pathologies are the angelic messengers.

A symbol is something that is "thrown together." Just as a potter throws clay on a wheel without knowing exactly what will emerge, this transitional vocation needs to allow for this unknown hiatus. "The characteristic of this area of transitional phenomena is the acceptance of the paradox that links external reality to inner experience."[6] In transition, there is a movement away from "either/or" perfectionistic thinking to a paradoxical attitude of "both/and." Depressive disintegration is accepted and encouraged in this time of trial, as all the pieces of priestly pathology are molded together and thrown into the fire of the kiln. The priesthood needs to embrace its own chaos.

The Old and the New

The pottery of the Pueblo Indians can serve as a helpful image here. When the clay is prepared for its formation, the Pueblos collect pottery shards from their land, that which was created by their ancestors. They grind these shards into a dust and combine them with the new clay.

Thus, the pottery contains something of the old, archetypal pots, and something of the new. These vessels serve as a connection with the past and a passage to the future, being both mediatory and transitional themselves. The same can be said for the priesthood. The disorders of priesthood may seem to be rare. However, these deviations have existed since its primitive life and are necessary to its very character. They need to be accepted in the kiln, the soul, of every priest, who can then be transformed through the fire that molds them into something new. Here, listen to the prayer of Isaiah for the return of God's favor: "We are the clay and you are the potter; we are all the work of your hands" (Isaiah 64:7; see also, Isaiah 29:16, and Jeremiah 18:6).

As the prophets knew, transitions hold mystery, contradiction, inconsistency, spontaneity, and ambiguity. These shifts are "potential space," says Arnold Modell,[7] which allow the interplay of inner psychic reality and external reality. "Transitional space is," as Winnicott stresses, "the site of play, creativity, and intimacy."[8] The psychopathological disorders of priesthood offer us a way into these potential spaces of initiation, where priests are being invited to enter into a process of transformation. We need to be creative, to play, to use our imaginations, and become intimately involved with these symptoms. Then, all of the fear and chaos can be contained and held in the potter's hand. Robert Moore describes this process as one that is essential to all human, personal, and social transformation.

> It is evident to me that apparent personal or social changes that occur outside a context of containment are usually, if not always, superficial in nature or abortive in consequences. Deep structural change requires a reliable psychosocial framing, the facilitation of a holding environment that can help individuals and groups to tolerate the terrors of change, with its attendant painful truths or emotions.[9]

A Holding Environment

The current experience of priesthood suggests that a "holding environment" of darkness, deficiency, and diminishment is where God may be discovered. This recognition of God's absence is absolutely necessary if the transformation of priesthood is to happen. The prophet

Jeremiah is a good example of one priest who discovers deep meaning in this experience of darkness. Just as he did, priests can enter this mysterious space through the symptoms of their psychological disorders. By embracing the emptiness, terror can be contained.

So, this transitional space is actually a time of contemplative prayer, "the epiphanic place for all images of the archetypal world."[10] Priests *can* discover meaning in their psychopathology by getting in touch with these primordial, contemplative symbols that speak of God's absence.

If we focus on the illnesses of priests only from a therapeutic perspective, it is not surprising that we might miss the mark, that we might not see God hidden away in the deeper realities of these disorders. By taking a more contemplative and mystical viewpoint, however, we may rediscover priesthood through this rather obscure discovery that God, the hidden God, dwells in these psychological disorders. Following this path from trial to transformation is to accept the "via negativa." What God hides, God also reveals. Let us enter the darkness and begin the journey.

CHAPTER TWO

From Darkness to Light

In the unconscious of all priests there is an archetype of priesthood, which ... they ignore at their own peril, for it belongs to their life, it is part of their destiny.[1]

The noted pioneer of psychology, C.G. Jung, postulated that religious belief in the modern world is being expressed through psychological symptoms.[2] In the contemporary world, he concluded, psychopathological disorders can lead us to understand the archetypes, or the original forms, upon which basic human patterns and needs are created. *Arche* means beginning, origin, cause, and supreme rule; type means image, form, norm, or prototype.

According to Jung, the archetypes reflect the contents of the collective unconscious, which he also called the objective psyche. As opposed to the personal unconscious, which is comprised of everything in the life of a person that has been forgotten or repressed, the objective psyche is "the inherited possibility of psychic functioning in general, i.e. in the inherited structure of the brain."[3] It can be compared to our genetic makeup, which goes back to the very first human being and carries us ahead into the future.

Jung says that the archetypes are the *Imago Dei*, the image of God, in a soul; the primordial forms that have existed since the remotest times.[4] The archetype of priesthood can be traced as far back as the beginnings of human civilization, far in advance of Christianity.[5] These primordial patterns are universal forms of behavior, centers of energy for the human psyche.[6] "The archetype is like a psychic mold into which individual and collective experiences are poured and where they take shape."[7] An archetype is "experienced emotionally as a personal call which harkens us back to the very roots of our human existence..., a giver of meaning."[8]

An Indelible Mark

Archetypes can be related to the theological proposition that the priesthood is an indelible mark. Since St. Augustine, Christian theology has held that a vocation to the priesthood leaves this seal on a person's soul (psyche).

> The idea of an indelible mark in the soul could correspond to a kind of priestly archetype or primordial imprint of what priesthood has always meant to human beings, being present in the psyche of certain people. Perhaps ordination could be seen as publicly recognizing this archetypal constellation in the person.[9]

I will point out again that priesthood can exist as an archetypal form in the lives of many people, not simply those who are recognized by institutional ordination. This prototype of priesthood has a numinous and transcendent quality that is beyond consciousness; an "eternal presence."[10] Because of this, its manifestation is not always apparent, even to the people who possess the mark.

The most characteristic feature of an archetype is its ambivalence, its potentiality for being either positive or negative.[11] And, it is within human experience to become trapped in the negative aspects of an archetype or to discover its healing promise. So, a priest could easily become entangled in pathologies without personal awareness. This is especially true today because we live in an age when these "disorders" carry negative connotations. Psychology and medicine want to rid us of symptoms. Using Jung's vocabulary, this would mean that the archetypes become more and more hidden from view. Therefore, their manifestations are kept secret. This is precisely what the church has done with the archetypal nature of priesthood. Acting out of fear, it has hidden psychological disorders under a veil of distinction. The essential elements of priesthood cannot therefore be discovered. The archetype of priesthood has been violated. Archetypes have an unconscious core of meaning:

> ...they are bringers of protection and salvation and their violation has as its consequence the perils of the soul ... Moreover, they are the unfailing causes of neurotic and even psychotic disorders, behaving exactly like neglected or maltreated physical organs or organic functional systems.[12]

Throughout this book, the trials of priesthood will represent the negative, disordered expression of this archetype, which has been hidden in the darkness. The trials require transformation if this vocation is to regain its proper place within the context of humanity.

Repressed and Neglected

Neglected archetypes are repressed (i.e. turned into unacceptable ideas, feelings, thoughts, behaviors, etc., and in the process are relegated to the unconscious and become inaccessible). They insist on restitution by possessing the ego. The archetypes, as Murray Stein observes, offer essential clues as to what the symptoms symbolize; they need to be honored or else they will erupt in psychopathological disturbances.[13]

The priesthood today certainly suffers from disregard. We need to ask: what is being repressed and neglected as the priesthood conceals these disorders? How do we dishonor the priesthood? How can we discover the redeeming hope that lies within these symptoms? Neglected archetypes need a religious cure; they are related to a "Preeminent Potential."

Psychological growth occurs only when one attempts to bring the content of the archetypes into conscious awareness and establish a relationship between one's conscious life and the archetypal level of human existence.[14]

The content of this unconscious repression is certainly apparent to us today in all of the problems that priests face. Like many archetypes which become too familiar, the priesthood is evolving into "banal superficiality."[15] Historically, it has taken on a strong persona enabling priests to develop powerful egos and "magical prestige."[16] Such a persona, says Jung, is "a mask of the collective psyche, a mask that feigns individuality, making others and oneself believe that one is individual ..."[17] With the lifting of this mask in the past thirty years (because of many factors both within the church and without), the priesthood is now challenged to rediscover its archetypal roots. "This confrontation is the first test of courage," says Jung,[18] because it requires that one encounter the shadow, the dark and negative side of an archetype.

The Secrets Are Out

This has certainly been the case in the last thirty years. The priesthood has suffered both indignities and shame. The media is filled with accounts of priests with psychological and psychosexual disorders. Priests have been leaving the active ministry in droves. Problems such as depression, low morale, anxiety, loneliness, confused sexuality, aggression, abuses of power, and struggles for control are now widely known to exist within the priesthood. Its shadow side is quite obvious.

Fear of this darkness leads to various responses. The strongest of these seems to be an effort at restoring the "good old days" of prominence and prestige, unoriginal and patriarchal dominance. This is a devious temptation (primarily because it stems from fear) to push the darkness down into the depths of the unconscious where the truth will, once again, be repressed. Fear also causes these disorders to be treated therapeutically and medically, with the hope of a cure, further separating the priesthood from any transformation. So, many priests are sent off to treatment centers and hospitals, where they seek healing and rehabilitation. What we seem to be missing, however, is the fact that God may very well be trying to transform the priesthood *through* these very disorders. Attempts at healing and curing may only be reinforcing the repression. The darkness shall be the light. The disease points to the cure.

As A.W. Richard Sipe expresses it in his book, *A Secret World: Sexuality and the Search for Celibacy,*[19] it may not be that these pathologies are new to the priesthood. It is true, however, that the veil of secrecy has been lifted concerning priestly symptoms. The problem is that we may be failing to see the real truth that is being uncovered.

Ignoring the Message

In covering up all of these disorders, we have not only caused them to become even stronger, we have also ignored their essential message: that the very archetype and core of priesthood can be uncovered in them! This is an even bigger secret that needs to be told. These "problems" can truly be a blessing in disguise, since we have now been brought face to face with the concealed shadow side of this vocation, the "agony in the garden"; the first step toward salvation. Spiritual poverty opens an archetype for renewal.

> Is there ... an unconscious pattern of behavior (or to use Jung's term, archetype) of the ministry? Is there a basic pattern of behavior which the priest must become conscious of in himself? Is there an archetypal image of the priest which can give a form to his ministerial interactions with others and with his own self? Is there an essential role which people have expected and have a right to expect from the priest?[20]

These are some of the questions that need to be addressed in the light of these priestly disorders. In an excellent summary of the psychological symptoms found in the clergy, Jack Bloom sees these characteristics as archetypal, in that they indicate a certain "set-apartness" in priests.

> That the clergy are a deviant group in American culture has been suggested by a great many observers ... A sense of differentness and otherness has endless references in the literature ... One might then hypothesize that the men who become religious professionals, who enter a world of differentness and otherness, do

so because of some strong personality determinants that may differentiate them from the rest of the population.[21]

The psychological disorders of priests can tell us what archetypal shadows are being ignored because of fear. I claim that by finding the meaning of these symptoms, the essence of the priesthood can be rediscovered. This will require the sacrifice of ego needs, however, because it is excessive ego control that causes the symptoms (archetypes) to be hidden in the darkness and therefore pathological.

As we enter into a new millennium, priests are challenged to end the deception that has led them to "lord it" over others, and come into the light. The buried seeds of these symptoms have the possibility of germinating into a true vocation. An archetypal analysis can bring the priesthood to rediscover its energy and life, its very soul. As William Dols explains, this crisis in the clergy is surfacing because

> The dominants that once nourished them are decaying. They experience increased restlessness from the center, and painful symptoms of depression (and) alcoholism discounted as midlife crises, to be weathered or solved by sabbaticals, additional staff, or a call to a new parish. What is ignored is an archetypal shift occurring in the Self ...[22]

Confronting the Shadow
If, in fact, the "heroic" priesthood is dying, we are entering a time of great potential grace and healing.

> Healing comes from our unguarded side, from where we are foolish and vulnerable. This is expressed in the idea of the wounded healer, who heals through his own wounds—or needs or call ... Compassion does not flow from the ego.[23]

I believe that many psychological disorders have a divine origin. The symptoms associated with priesthood can give us a real clue as to how its wounds can transform the priesthood and restore its ethical and upright place in society. This, though, is a painful process. "Confrontation with the shadow," says Jung, "produces at first a dead balance, ... everything becomes doubtful ... in this torn and divided state."[24] This is so because the ego must die. When ego dies, chaos ensues. This, by the way, includes institutional ego. Obviously, because of all of the problems that have surfaced concerning the priesthood, we seem to be in the midst of this "dead balance."

So, we are being called by this darkness to turn back, to revert to the archetypal origins of priesthood to accept metanoia. The role of priest is being humbled. But, as the archetypal psychologist James Hillman says, humility is the traditional mark of the soul, and symptoms humil-iate.[25] The very core of priesthood needs to continue being chastened. "Is it not at all unthinkable that God may use cracked and imperfect vessels ...?"[26]

It is mainly through the wounds in human life that the Gods enter (rather than through pronouncedly sacred or mystical events), because pathology is the most palpable manner of bearing wit-ness to the process beyond ego control and the insufficiency of the ego perspective.[27]

These ideas resonate with those of John of the Cross and other reformers who were proponents of the "via negativa" in Christian spir-ituality. In trying to discover the true meaning of our symptoms, we first of all need to submit to the darkness and illness that lie within; we need to proceed with resignation and humility.[28] This night is bright but the darkness is luminous. We can no longer ignore the void.

This does not, by the way, mean submission. Far from it! It means that priests can reconnect with humanity, with the human, the humus. These pathological disorders, which every authentic priest experi-ences, must be accepted and shouldered as a burdening cross if priest-hood is to recover its lost meaning. "Anyone who does not take up the cross and follow me cannot be my disciple" (Luke 14:27). It is in this state of absence, as the priesthood experiences its descent into hell, that we can begin to honor its archetypal roots. "You know, the soul is always being rediscovered through pathology."[29]

CHAPTER THREE

From Depression to Contemplative Emptiness

When we allow ourselves to fall into the depths, we do not plunge into mere emptiness. We fall into the height, whose height opens a depth.[1]

Today, priests are confronted with many issues that seem to threaten their traditional roles. These include questions about sexuality, celibacy and intimacy, the role of laypeople in ministry and leadership, the priest shortage, growing expectations in response to this shortage, loneliness, fear, and a lack of adequate support systems. It is not uncommon for priests to develop symptoms of depression. Some are manifested in connection with eating (sparse appetite or overeating). Others include poor concentration, sleep disturbances, low energy or hyperactivity, low self-esteem, and feelings of hopelessness. Depression can cause serious psychological turmoil. It also relates to the spiritual experience of the "dark night of the soul."

Many of the great saints have lived through what is called the "dark night of the soul." Many of the great religious mystics ... were suddenly shut away from God, their prayers empty. Service to their religion was an empty discipline. Life was empty. The sun did not shine as brightly, the spring was not as beautiful, nothing had the meaning, nothing had the intensity, nothing had the beauty it should have. What emerges from their accounts with great clarity is in actuality the picture of the classic depression. They felt depressed; they hated themselves. They felt completely hopeless and despondent, bad, useless, wasted. I feel that there are many clergymen like these.[2]

The ideas expressed here by Margaretta Bowers certainly have a negative ring to them. They were written in 1963, just as the Second Vatican Council was making its historic changes in the church, while there was still a plethora of priests in the United States. In our modern, psychological age, this experience of emptiness is called depression. However, many mystics who followed a "negative way," recognized many positive spiritual characteristics within it. The journey into darkness is a way toward uncovering the light.

A Common Disorder

The psychological illness called depression is frequently described as a common disorder in the lives of priests. In trying to face all of the current difficulties in their lives, priests often live with these symptoms: excessive worry, pessimism, irritability, dissatisfaction, a lack of self-confidence, withdrawal, insecurity, overly controlled attitudes, aloofness, unsociability, grief, self-deprecation, feelings of guilt, low psychic energy, existential angst, and lethargy. A conspicuous number of studies have been undertaken in the past thirty years to substantiate this idea that these manifestations have archetypal significance. As Bowers explains above, there is some historical verification that these symptoms have been experienced for a long time.

A probe commissioned in 1985 by the National Conference of Catholic Bishops, entitled *The Health of American Catholic Priests*, found that 35% of the priests interviewed said that they felt depressed often or sometimes.[3] In another recent analysis, after studying priests for twenty years, the Center for Human Development found that 62% of priests deny negative emotions such as anger and aggression (denial of anger is often associated with depression), 94% need to grow in self-directedness, 42% have lower than average or a complete lack of self-esteem, and 47% felt negativity toward themselves.[4]

Clergy are often found to be more submissive, introspective, worrisome, isolated, withdrawn, dependent, and self-conscious than comparable lay populations.[5] Studying clergy from the perspective of depth psychology, Mark Kane found them to be isolated, insecure, and conforming.[6] Of course, all of these characteristics can be included in the symptoms of depression.

Many studies that have been conducted on priests using the Minnesota Multiphasic Personality Inventory (MMPI), a common psychological test, show that priests are high on the depression scale.[7] In addition, it does not appear that these high levels of depression result simply from being a Roman Catholic. A study which compared Catholic college freshmen to Protestants discovered that the Catholic students had lower depression scales on this psychological test (the MMPI) than the Protestants.[8] In this and in other studies, depression does appear to be more common in priests than in laypeople. In severe cases it can be debilitating:

> The religious who is so afflicted gives up all interest in living and, as a consequence, fails to care for the ordinary needs of life. He will sit in his room by the hour in mute silence. He seems oblivious to the comforting remarks of his fellow religious. He can see nothing good in himself or in his past life. He feels that he has been a total failure. He sees no use in trying to continue in the religious state. Frequently he despairs of saving his soul ... A psychotic depression is more apt to strike a religious in the middle-forties or later rather than in the earlier years of religious life ... A psychotic depression is not a spiritual problem, even though the element of despair may be present.[9]

Once again, we see depression described in a psychological framework, and rightly so. It is certain that a psychotic depression can lead to very serious problems such as total withdrawal and suicide. Clinical depression is also associated with other psychopathological and physical illnesses. It should never be trivialized or ignored, or merely labeled as a mood or as a "rite of passage." Psychotropic medications can be very effective in treating depression along with therapeutic intervention.

A Deeper Meaning

At the same time, however, a deeper meaning can be discerned in this disorder. The symptoms of depression can teach us a great deal about the depth and the archetypal soul of priesthood, and this is the notion that will be pursued here. A study trying to find a correlation between burnout and depression among 239 Catholic priests, 94% of whom were diocesan priests concludes:

> the priest who tends to become overloaded, and is introverted, may be more susceptible than other priests to burnout and depression. Furthermore, reliance more upon feelings to cope with stress than logical, cognitive coping styles may also lead to burnout and depression.[10]

The symptoms for burnout and depression are quite similar.[11] "Burned-out priests were therefore characterized by internal and external overload, reduced attention, impulsiveness, obsessiveness, negative affect expression and introversion."[12]

> 10.46% of the priests in this sample were highly burned out, 54.39% moderately burned out, and 35.15% showed low burnout ... Personal prayer and agreement with the Church's teachings were associated with low degree of burnout. Priests who reported using more time for spiritual reading and solitude reported experiencing more personal accomplishment and less depression than other priests. Using a support group did not seem to make a difference between being burned out or not.[13]

We can begin to notice here a connection being made between spiritual interests—prayer, contemplation, and upholding tradition—and lower depression rates in priests. As we will see later, all of these characteristics are associated with the archetypal images of priesthood. In another study of burnout among 434 priests of the Diocese of Albany, New York, the author found that "deficiency of self-actualization correlated highly with burnout." He also concluded that "a resistance to intimacy was a significant predictor of ... burnout."[14]

A document issued by the U.S. Catholic Bishops, *Reflections on the Morale of Priests*, seems to succinctly describe depression among priests:

> They fear that their youthful hopes and dreams will never be achieved; that the vision they had seems to be slipping away or is unimportant now; that there is no possibility of the rewards or recognition once dreamed of; that they will not be replaced; that they will be left quite alone; and, perhaps most significant of all, they feel that they have little or no control over their lives and future.[15]

Group Art Therapy

Not long ago, I conducted a retreat for a group of priests from a Diocese in the South. During one of the sessions I invited these men to engage in a group art therapy project. I spread out a white sheet of paper on a large table. I told the priests that their task was to design their diocese on this paper by drawing anything that they felt the diocese needed. This was a prime opportunity, I explained to them, to have all of their dreams fulfilled (at least in an imaginary way)! I gave them colored markers and told them that the only requirement was that they work together.

Of course, many things can be learned about a group from a projective drawing like this one. To enlighten the discussion here concerning depression, however, two images in this group drawing were overwhelming. These priests drew dinosaurs and cemeteries. The dinosaurs were very large, dominating the drawing. Cemeteries outnumbered any other images.

In the discussion that followed, we were all somewhat dazed by what had been produced. The unconscious of this group seemed to be expressing a type of depression, a preoccupation with death. Was this because of a certain wish and desire, or was it because of external forces which threatened death? In the discussion we learned that both were true. These priests were feeling great pressure from external circumstances; morale was low. However, they also seemed to share an unconscious death wish and a desire for renewal from the "bones and ashes" of these dinosaurs and cemeteries.

> Through depression we enter depths and in depths find soul. Depression is essential to the tragic sense of life. It moistens the dry soul and dries the wet. It brings refuge, limitation, focus, gravity, weight, and humble powerlessness. It reminds of death. The true revolution (in behalf of soul) begins in the individual who can be true to his or her depression.[16]

Following Its Direction

Depression can be understood as a withdrawal of psychic energy from consciousness. According to Jung, we need to follow the direction indicated by a depression in order to experience salvation.[17] Melancholia (an old term used to describe depression) is a remedy for the afflictions of the soul. "As their purses shrank (through depression) their soul gained in stature."[18] The encounter with depression is, however, an experience of chaos, a confrontation with the shadow and darkness which lies within. Depression is a blackening which can be the first step toward liberation.[19] It is a "great religious crisis,"[20] the way in which God afflicts the senses.[21]

> A person in depression ... is unconsciously living the archetype of death and rebirth. Depressed people often try to distract themselves or pull themselves out of it. But if they do that, the death is not experienced fully and the rebirth part of the process may not occur. They must recognize that there is a good reason for the depression and that they can help themselves by trying to understand it.[22]

The Latin word *depressare* means to press down hard. Depression is associated with a type of descent. I propose that we picture it as God pressing the priest down so that the true vocation can be discovered. "Being down is a part of life."[23] The Psalms of the Hebrew Scriptures, which priests pray in the Liturgy of the Hours, continually allude to this descent (cf. Psalms 69, 73, 115:17). "Though you have made me feel many bitter afflictions, you will again revive me; from the depths of the earth you will once more raise me" (Psalm 71:20).

> Only the one who has accepted this process of mystical death, who has undertaken the soul's journey to the other side and withstood the voyage on the night sea, into hell ("traveled down into the realm of the dead"), can stand before his fellow men (and women) with this experience as one changed, even as a "new person," and bring them the knowledge of new life.[24]

This is precisely why depression is a valuable sign of the indelible mark, or archetype, of priesthood. A priest, as mediator, can make use of the experience of this "dark death" in order to mediate and help others emerge from similar descents. The priest's depression is related to contemplation, to a "dark night," to the interior life. It is part of an initiation rite into the vocation of priesthood. One is reminded of Dante's *Inferno*. Depression, then, can be described as a *decensus ad inferos*. Descent implies a deepening, a journey into the interior of one's soul; inward and downward! A priest needs to be carried inward, into the emptiness.

Priesthood has sacrificial, prophetic, and messianic qualities inherent in its archetypal form.[25] The disorder that we call depression, when viewed within the framework of these three images, can give us a deeper understanding apart from a mere medical interpretation. The words that we use to describe depression may allow for these buried symbols to emerge. "Do you not know that words are eggs," asks the Jungian analyst, Russell Lockhart, "that words carry life, that words give birth?"[26] After receiving this message in a dream, Lockhart began a quest to break open the shell of words by paying attention to their etymological roots. In this way, the hidden soul of words is expressed.[27]

His advice will be heeded in this book in an attempt to unearth the hidden meaning of priestly depression. I would like to do this by looking at three classical roles of priests: messianic, prophetic, and sacrificial.

1. A Messianic Attitude

Originally, the term king was used in this context (priest, prophet, and king). Kingship is a term with negative associations in our democratic world. In the scriptures, however, the king is associated with the messiah and savior.[28] Throughout Judeo-Christian history the concept of the king/messiah has a particular meaning. For one thing, this messiah does not maintain all of the trappings that are usually associated with royalty. In addition, the messianic salvation will be one of universal peace, not domination.

Messianism also carries the message of forgiveness and reconciliation and it reveals hidden truth. Universal peace and human integrity are its fruits, and unity is preserved only by accepting diversity. The acts that inaugurate the messianic time are never seen as political, but as the work of God, often accomplished through the agency of a minister. All of this calls for a mediator who is receptive and acts on behalf of God's intervention, and this is in contradiction to ego power or prestige.

Some of the symptoms of depression seem to fit within the framework of this messianic mediation. Worry, for example, is a messianic attribute. The word "worry" loosely means "binding tightly." Certainly, it is within the function of the priest to bind. In the Gospel of John, binding is associated with the gift of forgiveness: "Then he breathed on them and said: 'Receive the Holy Spirit. If you forgive the sins of people they are forgiven them; if you hold them bound, they are held bound'" (John 20:22–23).[29] This passage was interpreted by the Council of Trent to mean that priests could mediate God's Spirit on behalf of the community by forgiving sins in the sacrament of penance (reconciliation).

Undoubtedly, as priests hear the confessions of people, they must worry and experience a "bind." Holding all of this weakness and sorrow in one's heart is a true burden. Priests are also bound by the "seal of the confessional," which means that they can never divulge this information. In our contemporary world, this obligation is being challenged in courts and through litigation, causing a further sense of worry. How can priests help but worry about wounds that become bound up, their own and those of others? Excessive worry, however, can lead to a negative manifestation of this archetype, which becomes expressed as moralism and binding too tightly. Priests can misuse this power by keeping people bound to scrupulous and rigid beliefs.

The Need for Forgiveness

On the other hand, this grace of binding and being held bound is related to flexibility, openness, and understanding. The transformation of worry from a painful symptom to a positive symbol requires a messianic attitude. "Then Peter came up to ask him, 'Lord, when another wrongs me, how often must I forgive? Seven times?' 'No,' Jesus replied, 'not seven times; I say, seventy times seven times'" (Matthew 18:21–22). This biblical conversation expresses a true description of messianic peace. Forgiveness is infinite. We live in a culture where revenge and litigation abound. If this cultural conditioning becomes too overpowering, a priest can be tempted to excessive worry, which eventually finds its expression in moralistic judgmentalism and authoritarian anger, sure signs of the negative aspects of this archetypal disorder called depression.

Remaining bound to messianic forgiveness requires belief in a potential greater than that which is humanly possible. The healing associated with worry comes from knowing that God provides the forgiveness, even when a sin is repeated over and over again. The duty of a priest is to accept this belief in relation to self, and mediate this reconciliation on behalf of the community and God, continually binding the wounds of a sinner, seventy times seven.

Depression can be a transitional seasoning where a priest can enter into "the ordeal of enduring intense affect."[30] Edinger states that it is that aspect of the ego which is identified with transpersonal power that needs to undergo a process of penance and reconciliation.[31] Priests need to do penance for their excessive binding. This is experienced as a type of fire; a burning in the heart of the priest for penance, conversion, and transformation. Ego becomes vulnerable in this process, which will carry with it all of the symptoms of depressive disorder. Silence and a plea for mercy are the disposition a priest needs to take. Mercy is associated with the Latin word, *mare*, meaning sea, and the plea for mercy prepares a priest for initiation, the immersion into the transforming baptismal water once again.

Though fire and water are at war,
life's origins awake discordant harmonies
that move the entire world.[32]

Depression can therefore be a sign that the priest needs to develop greater forgiveness for self and others. Forgiveness necessitates that one's own ego be submissive. Excessive worry is transformed by the application of mercy and forgiveness.

Preservers of Tradition

The manifestation of over-control is another depressive symptom that fits within the messianic symbol. Control is associated with the word *rota*, a public road or a regular course upon which people travel. It is also connected to the word "rote," meaning repetition.

Priesthood has a messianic function of preserving tradition. Anamnesis, recalling and actualizing the sacred events of history, is central to messianism. In our constantly changing culture this idea is not always readily accepted.

Priests can be tempted to pathological control and the negative aspects of this archetype can be manifested in authoritarian excesses: rigidity, abuses of power, obduracy, and hardheartedness. It is imperative that priests begin to uphold tradition, in its truest sense. This has nothing to do with the political ideas of conservatism or liberalism. Rather, tradition here means "to hand on." It is the duty of a priest to hand over and to hand on the messianic message. Again, the activity of mediation is paramount.

This "handing on" is related to the messianic quality because it offers people a stable, regular course, one that has been traveled many times before, an archetypal and repetitive journey. Priests uphold this tradition by calling attention to the fact that we have ancestors, history, and a spiritual heritage which enables us to live as we do. Many saints have gone before us and remain a part of us (some of them even considered "sinners" in their time).

Priests who are honest with themselves and aware of their own authoritarianism and their excessive need to control every aspect of life and ministry, are being given a hidden grace. To respond to it, they need to get in touch with the deep roots of Life. Priests can mediate this message concerning regularity, repetition, and remembrance only if they themselves have discerned these connections in their own lives. This requires a familiarity with the great diversity, variety, and numerous paradoxes that are communicated in scripture, tradition, the lives of our ancestors (saints and sinners), and contemporary experiences. As mediator, a priest needs to be acclimated to the variety of transitions that bring us from one generation to another, the great diversity of thought over the centuries, and the wonderful "craziness" of so many saints. Then a priest is able to ritualize the deeper meanings of these events for other people. Without this familiarity, rigid dogmatism and authoritarianism, a desire to hold onto the past and interpret it as being static, take over as a defensive compensation, and the negative archetypal manifestations of depression will prevail. This is not true messianism. If this happens, a priest will need to engage in a great interior battle to let go of authoritarian control in favor of the messianic message: being a receptive mediator and instrument through whom tradition is handed on.

The Symptom of Withdrawal

The image of messiah can also be associated with the depressive symptom called withdrawal. We see in this word the need to draw back, to go back. Depressive drawing back can be revealed in two ways, either as a negative disassociation from people or as a movement toward mysticism. As Russian mystical writer Nicolas Berdyaev says,

> Mysticism gives vitality and spirit to the sources and the roots of all religious life. Mysticism is the essential basis of all religious consciousness; the hidden source of religion in the world. Religion carries over into life and consciousness what has been immediately experienced in mysticism ... The dogmas stiffen and become deformed into external authority when their mystical sources are closed.[33]

If a priest becomes more and more isolated from people in an effort to escape, the possibility of becoming overly dogmatic is very real. However, if the withdrawal is aligned with mysticism, then a priest is driven to relate intimately.

When a priest responds positively to the archetypal need to be solitary, an awareness of integrity becomes possible. In fact, it is this uniqueness that opens one up to authentic relationship. "It is only as I am connected to my own core that I am connected to others."[34] This is what St. Benedict meant by stability, says Esther De Waal. It is a form of self-acceptance, "standing still in my own center."[35] This, she continues, is also related to an ability to live with diversity and change in life. "We need to accept that we are all different."[36] This acceptance can transform withdrawal and isolation into a messianic vision, where relationships are opened up and universality (catholicity) is embraced.

As stated earlier, messianism seeks a universal peace; it endeavors to preserve unity in the midst of diversity. The soul of the world, *anima mundi*, yearns for sustenance and liberation. This is one function of priesthood, and it is a solitary adventure. Solitude and relationship are a paradoxical diversity inherent in priesthood. In contemporary times, this vocation needs to be both related and isolated in many extents, from environmental awareness to the microcosm of each individual heart.

The Symptom of Apathy

The last symptom I want to mention in connection with a messianic attitude is the depressive symptom called lethargy. This word finds its significance in the term latent, which means "to lie hidden," and in *lethagos*, which means "forgetful."

It is not an essentially negative term. Scripture says that when the messiah comes no one is supposed to know his origins (John 7:27).

> The messiah would be hidden; for people would not know where he would come from, and he could stand in their midst without their knowing it.[37]

The messiah stands daily in our midst and we do not know it. It would be impossible for a priest to reveal the entirety of messianic truth. The symptom of lethargy implies limitation. A priest cannot reveal all the truth. Some aspects of truth will always be hidden. But some aspects of it are revealed in men and women all around us. The work of the messiah is not the work of the priest alone. Any priest who plays the role of savior, and is not aware of this boundary, will certainly experience the negative aspects of phlegmatic depression sooner or later.

As the old saying goes, forgetfulness is a necessary element of forgiveness. In order for this symptom to be transformed, priests need to forget themselves, lose themselves in the great "sea of humanity." Lethargy is a messianic gift that lies hidden within the priesthood. Priests can invite the people of the world to forgive and forget, to honor one another's traditions, to seek liberation and peace together. In this way, the messianic symptom of depression is honored and priests no longer need to carry all of the deadly archetypal weight.

2. A Prophetic Attitude

The prophetic function of priesthood can also be discerned in some of the characteristics of depression. As biblical scholar Walter Bruggeman puts it, "Prophetic ministry seeks to penetrate the numbness to face the body of death in which we are caught."[38]

Prophets are commonly known to be irritating, which is a symptom of this disorder. Prophets tend to arouse strong feelings within people, both positive and negative. In its negative manifestation, irritability comes across as meanness and cruelty. Jeremiah and Ezekiel, two of the priest-prophets of the Hebrew Scriptures, certainly experienced this irascible side of depression.

> Woe to me, mother, that you gave me birth! A man of strife and contention to all the land! ... Under the weight of your hand I sat alone because you filled me with indignation. Why is my pain continuous, my wound incurable, refusing to be healed? (Jeremiah 15:10, 17–18).

Ezekiel, in his vision of the dry bones, expresses the transformation that can take place from the death of irritable depression through the sign of the opening of the graves (Ezekiel 37). The word "irritable" is associated with the word "animate." If a priest is not animating people with the prophetic message, then the priest's own irritability will become overwhelming in a pathological way. On the other hand, this symptom can develop into a real blessing, mediating enthusiasm and zest for life.

When Anxiety Is Selfish

Insecurity is another symptom of depression which can be classified as a prophetic attribute. Paradoxically, insecurity is related to not having enough anxiety or care. Being insecure may reveal excessive ego focus. If priests are insecure and focused too much on their own egos, it is a sure sign that they may not be caring enough for others.

My experience as a spiritual director and therapist for priests for over twenty years tells me that many priests are often more interested in their own security than they are in caring for others. This is especially true because of the current problems surrounding priesthood. It can be seen in the accumulation of material things, in not wanting to be disturbed at certain times during a day, or in basic laziness. A need for security can be a way of avoiding anxiety. On the other hand, caring for people in a prophetic way causes positive anxiety, the kind that animates.

A friend of mine who is pastor of a large parish recently told me a story that applies here. Two priests serve as associates in his parish (this is obviously a large diocese). One day the pastor received a phone call from the hospital asking for a priest because a young child was dying. This child's parents wanted to see a priest, and the hospital chaplain was not available. Since the pastor was on his way to a special liturgy, he explained the situation and asked one of these two priests, both of whom were watching television, to go to the hospital. When he returned from the liturgy he found both priests still watching a football game. Neither of them had gone to the hospital. When he asked them why, they said that they checked the records and this family had not attended Mass there for some time. This being the case, they didn't feel that it was their obligation to care for them.

This is an example of the need for prophetic anxiety, which means "to cause pain." These two priests need to experience some anxious suffering so that they can learn greater care and compassion. Otherwise, they are both setting themselves up for a brush with pathological depression. In fact, some encounter with their own pain will create just the anxiety they need. God will eventually "press them down" so that they can be fermented into a new awareness.

The Importance of Being Aloof

Being aloof, another depressive symptom, fits with this prophetic stance. The word aloof comes from "luff" which is the behavior of a flapping sail when it is pointed too directly in the wind and fails to catch the air and move the boat forward. Metaphorically, priests are called to help people set or change the course of life. This word also suggests the windward side of an island. This is the face or side toward which the wind blows. Aloofness can be blown away if a priest accepts a prophetic role in the community. In a countercultural way, the course of society can be altered. Depression can do this; it can serve as the catalyst for a conversion into this prophetic vocation.

> What is it, in the end, that induces a man to go his own way? What is it, then, that inexorably tips the scales in favor of the extra-ordinary? It is what is commonly called vocation. Vocation acts like a law of God from which there is no escape. The original meaning of "to have a vocation" is "to be addressed by a voice." The clearest examples of this are to be found in the avowals of the Old Testament prophets.[39]

To be distant means to stand apart. Prophets are set apart. A prophetic priest will be different. Set-apartness means that a prophetic minister will not be bound by a secure, comfortable, and confident existence. Prophetic depression has the function of disengaging one from the safety of a self-possessed and unscathed existence. Depressive insecurity is overcome through concern and care for others, no matter what personal security needs to be sacrificed. "It is the task of prophetic ministry and imagination to bring people to engage their experiences of suffering to death."[40]

Prophetic ministry constantly brushes the insecurity of death and its paradoxical partner, life. The priesthood needs this anxiety. In his groundbreaking book *The Denial of Death*, Ernest Becker reminds us,

> The terrible guilt feelings of the depressed person are existential, that is, they represent the failure to live one's own life, to fulfill one's own potential because of the twisting and turning to be "good" in the eyes of the other. The other calls the tune to one's

eligibility for immortality, and so the other takes up one's unlived life.[41]

Prophets have unique personalities. Every priest needs to take heed of this life-giving potential and enter into the angst of life. In this way, the archetype is served and the integrity of the priestly vocation is reinforced.

Call to be Countercultural

Prophets are unsociable, which is also a symptom of depression. To be unsociable is to be released from allegiance to a society, a culture, or an organized group. In fact, the prophetic message often stands in opposition to collective mores. Priests today, being too enamored by complacent life-styles, by the expectations of authority figures, by the politics of our time, by over-acquisition and a desire for power, need to engage in a countercultural ethic. Perhaps this unsociable symptom is an invitation for priests to be liberated and unbound from the shackles of these cultural stereotypes. This challenge, too, applies to the church in general, which has, in many ways, aligned itself with the politically powerful and the elite. As Becker says in his initial remarks:

Religion is no longer valid as a hero system, and so the youth scorn it. If traditional culture is discredited as heroics, then the church that supports that culture automatically discredits itself. If the church, on the other hand, chooses to insist on its own special heroics, it might find that in crucial ways it must work against the culture, recruit youths to be anti-heroes to the ways of life of the society they live in. This is the dilemma of religion in our time.[42]

Unsociability would call priests to move beyond this socialization and away from collective pressures to conform, especially with the confines of institutional and cultural conditioning.

One Who Inspires Hope

"Abandon hope ye who enter here."[43] These words from Dante's immortal classic, *The Inferno,* depict the symptom of despair that can also accompany prophetic depression. Hope is gone.

Depression goes down. Hope, on the other hand, indicates opportunity, promise, belief, and desire. The prophetic role of a priest should inspire hope. Hope only has meaning, however, because of a seasoning in hopelessness. So, the current low morale and lack of ambition in the priesthood may be viewed as a precursor to this prophetic gift. "Prophetic ministry seeks to penetrate despair so that new futures can be believed in and embraced by us. There is a yearning for energy in a world grown weary."[44]

A familiar passage from the prophet Isaiah, which Jesus offers as the sign of the arrival of the messianic era and of his ministerial role (Luke 4:18–19), is pertinent here. After his experience in the desert, where he is tempted and shows his disdain for a role that would abuse political power, Jesus enters the temple and is prepared to begin his preaching. He dramatically opens the scriptures and begins to read:

> The spirit of the Lord God is upon me, because the Lord has anointed me; he has sent me to bring glad tidings to the lowly, to heal the brokenhearted, to proclaim liberty to captives and release to the prisoners, to announce a year of favor from the Lord and a day of vindication by our God, to comfort all who mourn; to place on those who mourn in Zion a diadem instead of ashes, to give them the oil of gladness instead of mourning, a glorious mantle instead of a listless spirit. They will be called oaks of justice, planted by the Lord to show his glory (Isaiah 61:1–3).

Certainly, depression is directly confronted by this message, which fully explains the prophetic priestly role. Isaiah is announcing the Jubilee year in Judaism. Jesus sees himself as fulfilling this text for all time. This scripture passage can be the threshold of a modern vocation to the priesthood, as it was for the ministry of Jesus. Without its prophetic significance the priesthood is meaningless and thus in despair and without hope. True prosperity and security lie in liberating, releasing, vindicating, and restoring.

3. A Sacrificial Attitude

The sacrificial quality of priesthood has to do with woundedness. One of its wounds is pessimism, a trait of depression that is connected to impairment, injury, and limitation. Pessimism is associated with the "incurable wound" of Jeremiah mentioned above (cf. Jeremiah 15:18). Many priests today are not in touch with their own woundedness and affliction. This archetypal idea recognizes that one who serves in this capacity is both sacrificer and sacrificed. As many spiritual authors have testified, the priest is both wounded and a healer.

However, when a priest is not in touch with personal woundedness there is a strong likelihood that the pain will be projected onto those who are being served. If a priest does not recognize the sacrificial element inherent in this vocation, then it is likely that the negative aspects of this archetype will be acted out. If so, a priest may express the pessimistic arrogance of seeing wounds in everyone else.

The positive dimension of this archetype will be apparent when a priest is able to offer his own ego to be sacrificed. Priests are called to mediate the woundedness of all humanity. If a priest begins to believe that he is immune to illness, woundedness, sin, and sickness, then a type of depression will most likely ensue, with its accompanying pessimism and hopelessness!

Pain and Sacrifice

The symptom of "dissatisfaction" also presents images having to do with the sacrificial charism. This word derives from feeling "sad." It has penitential connotations. Depression can come upon a priest when penance is not a familiar personal experience. This also has associations with pain and sacrifice. When a priest is aware of personal suffering, guilt (another symptom of depression), and sin, then healing can be offered to others in a ministerial manner. Without this appreciation, a priest is likely to become unforgiven: self-righteous, arrogant, dissatisfied, and depressed.

Grief is heaviness. It suggests that one takes a weight upon oneself. The Good Shepherd (cf. John 10:1–18) is an image of this aspect of priestly vocation.

Come to me all you who are weary and find life burdensome, and I will refresh you. Take my yoke upon your shoulders and learn from me, for I am gentle and humble of heart. Your soul will find rest, for my yoke is easy and my burden light (Matthew 11:28–30).

In our fashionable age, when issues like codependency are so strong in "pop" psychology, this may not seem like a very healthy notion.[45] In truth, we *are* dependent upon one another, even though it doesn't always fit within our independently minded culture.[46] Perhaps this is another place where priesthood becomes countercultural. Priests may need to mediate the grief that comes about when people become either overly independent or overly dependent. In our society, almost every family, system, and institution can be labeled "dysfunctional."

Actually, this is *the* gospel that we all need to embrace. There really is no person or system that can be defined as functional, because creation thrives on diversity. The human condition is disordered, because this is life! No one person can exemplify order; life is a vastly varying reality. So, it becomes the duty of priesthood to authenticate this fact and mediate this truth for the world. The more we destroy diversity, the less chance the whole creation has of surviving. (This is why it is so important, for example, to save the rain forests. By destroying them, we continually lose more and more diversity, and thus, life itself. The same can be said for humanity.)

Developing Compassion

This sacrificial ministry might also help alleviate the depressive symptom of grief in priests. Certainly, an encounter with grief can help develop compassion for the loss, the pain, and the suffering of others, which may be "codependence," but is nonetheless following a sacrificial vocation.

It is said that priests express a certain intrapunitive symptom when depressed. This word evokes images of turning pain inward. Also, it is associated with "pining." So, there is a yearning and a desire on the part of priests to internalize pain. Perhaps the priesthood today is not pining enough, not yearning for the sacrifice that is a real sign of its purpose. This is expanded negatively when priests engage in a type of unconscious masochistic expiation, seeing themselves as victims and martyrs, which is not authentic sacrifice.

Being intrapunitive can be transformed through repentance, regret, and expiation. The priesthood is challenged to take responsibility for its own woundedness, pain, and suffering so that it can begin to bear the burdens of sacrificial life. Priesthood has an obligation to mediate this message to others: that we all need to take personal responsibility for our own lives! In a codependent age, where people are encouraged to be disconnected victims, this message clearly has a prophetic ring. Being attached to others requires sacrifice. When loss and personal accountability are accepted, the intrapunitive aspects of depression will begin to be transformed.

The Need for Prayer

Finally, priesthood needs a greater immersion in prayer and meditation. The depressive symptoms of introspection, introversion, silence, and self-deprecation are associated with this sacrificial need.

Silence means "to say nothing." It is related to the image in "quietly flowing water."[47] Priesthood is aligned with this baptismal symbolism. "If anyone thirsts, let that person come to me and drink. Who believes in me, scripture has it: 'From within this one rivers of living water shall flow'" (John 7:37–38). There is no need to speak when this image is alive in a priest. The life of priesthood will flow through example, from within the silence.

Introspection can lead a priest to turn within; this is contemplation. Priesthood needs sacrificial contemplation because this is exactly where the self-deprecation can be confronted. Deprecate means "to avert by prayer."[48] If priests are not engaging in contemplative prayer then this self-deprecating aspect of depression can become overwhelming, finding expression in negative archetypal disorders, such as workaholism, perfectionism, and, of course, depression. Self-condemnation is averted by the self-reflection of turning within.

I maintain that the empty prayers, the empty discipline, and the empty life can be symbolically meaningful as signs of the messianic, prophetic, and sacrificial roles that comprise this vocation. In this empty posture, a priest can realize the depth that directs this vocation: a still, calm, peaceful, simple, unpretentious, and comforting potential presence guiding life and ministry, a "still, small voice."

> The gesture of a gift is adequate.
> If you have nothing: laurel leaf nor bay,
> no flower, no seed, no apple gathered late,
> do not in desperation lay

the beauty of your tears upon the clay.

No gift is proper to a Deity;
no fruit is worthy for such power to bless.
If you have nothing, gather back your sigh,
and with you hands held high, your heart held high,
lift up your emptiness![49]

Faith and Darkness

All of this brings us to the meaning of *via negativa* as expressed by many Christian mystics. Faith is a real darkness. Depression and low morale can be seen as incentives toward deeper faith. "Faith ... is a dark night for a person, but in this very way it gives light. The more darkness it brings upon a person, the more light it sheds. For by blinding it illumines ..."[50] Accordingly, a powerful ego, which can be commonly ascertained in priests as a cover-up for depression, must be emptied if faith is to have a real life. "For you darkness itself is not dark, and night shines as the day" (Psalm 139:12).

This negative theology contains the real message that lies hidden underneath priestly depression. Many of the mystics who put forth this *via negativa* were reformers of the church and of her clergy. Meister Eckhart, an advocate of this "school of letting go," says that it is by active cooperation and by passive contemplation that the second Birth takes place in the soul.[51] Depression is a descent into darkness which can be a preparation to honor the soul of priesthood. Priests must stop denying this deflation and enter into the emptiness with a deep conviction that it can initiate their true vocation.

"Epiphany accompanies darkness."[52] This ambivalent image is at the core of understanding priestly depression. Animation, life, and rebirth flow directly from the symptomatic waters of this disorder. Depression, says Jung, can be seen most clearly "in the empty stillness which precedes creative work."[53]

The most powerful prayer, and almost the strongest of all to obtain everything, and the most honorable of all works, is that which proceeds from an empty spirit ... An empty spirit is one that is confused by nothing, attached to nothing, has not attached its best to any fixed way of acting, and has no concern whatever in anything for its own gain, for it has all sunk down into God's dearest will and has forsaken its own.[54]

The psychological disorder called depression has within it the possibility of initiating one into the indelible mark of this vocation. Priests only need to freely enter its shadowy depths to discover the messianic, prophetic, and sacrificial aspects of this dark and illuminating archetype. Depression is a grace that can bring a priest to the threshold of understanding the limitations and imperfections of being human.

CHAPTER FOUR

From Being Perfect
to Living with Imperfection

**Let us return to imperfection's school
No longer wandering after Plato's ghost.[1]**

Over the past 20 years, whenever I would talk about perfectionism to groups of priests, I would invariably be approached by participants commenting: "I was amazed, I actually thought that you were reading a personal description of my life!" Here is a retelling of that characterization.

Perfectionistic priests have the following obsessive-compulsive fears and symptoms:[2] they are highly competitive, excessively achievement oriented, impatient, easily frustrated, preoccupied with deadlines, and have a tendency to react defensively to criticism. Perfectionist priests have a self-disclosure phobia because they believe that confession of their inner ideas and feelings might cause them to appear foolish, weak, or inadequate, and these deficiencies do not fit the idealization of priesthood. This fear prevents priests from enjoying warm and intimate companionship. On the other hand, "one of the catastrophes that perfectionists dread is rejection."[3] This conjunction of the fear of intimacy and the fear of rejection is a real archetypal motif that is associated with priesthood.

The distorted symptoms that accompany this sort of obsessive-compulsive disorder also include the following. First, these priests have what is called "all-or-nothing thinking." Everything is either black or white. A perfectionist priest fears mistakes and will overreact to them, possibly interpreting them in terms of sin rather than mere human limitation. Since idealization has been fostered in priestly formation, communicating a message that priests are "special," any experience of common humanity can be shunned as evil. This type of perception, then, can lead to many forms of prejudice, where extremes of thought and belief take over. It can also result in living at the extremes of the dependent/independent continuum, being submissive to authority figures, while, at the same time, stubborn and authoritarian toward others.

Over-generalization is another common symptom of this malady. There is a tendency on the part of these priests to jump to negative conclusions that the same mistakes will be made over and over again. "I'm always making this mistake. I'll never change; I'll never get it right!" So, forgiveness can slowly but surely be eroded and become irrelevant. There is a narrow margin of safety in this type of thinking. Reconciliation does not have a real and permanent impact in the lives of these priests.

The Need for Self-Compassion

"I should have done that right." "I should never have made that decision." "I ought to know better, I'm a priest." "I should be a better person." "I shouldn't get angry." "I should have worked harder." These priests continually berate themselves, having very little self-compassion. Ironically, however, they have no desire to learn from their mistakes.

This affects their interaction and ministry with others, since a perfectionist priest can become compulsively moralistic. Andrew Samuels calls this a "morality of narcissism" which really indicates "an addiction to perfection."[4] These same "shoulds" eventually become applied to others.

The "saint or sinner syndrome" has strong applications in the lives of these priests. The first time one lapses from a rigorous routine, the period of "sainthood" ends and a compensatory reaction of sin ensues. This is commonly seen in relation to sexuality, but also in other attempts to stop particular feelings or behavior. The period of "sin" is then accompanied by binges, moralistic self-deprecation and a long period of guilt, which only leads to further acting out in an effort to ease the pain of guilt. "If I'm no good anyway, why not do as I please?" It is a malignant cycle.

This disorder is obviously self-defeating. An obsessive-compulsive priest will become trapped by nonproductive rumination and self-critical ideas. The feelings of defeat turn into self-fulfilling prophecies. Thus, priests cannot produce adequate work because they become compulsive and obsess about every little thought, feeling, or behavior. David Burns describes six disadvantages that one of his patients listed concerning perfectionism:

> One, it makes me so tight and nervous I can't produce fine work or even adequate work at times. Two, I am often unwilling to risk the mistakes necessary to come up with a creative piece of work. Three, my perfectionism inhibits me from trying new things and making discoveries because I am so preoccupied with being "safe." Thus, my world becomes narrow and somewhat boring, and I lose out on the opportunity for new challenges. Four, it makes me self-critical and takes the joy out of life. Five, I can't even relax because I'll always find something that isn't perfect. Six, it makes me intolerant of others because I am constantly aware of the errors people make, and I end up being perceived as a fault-finder.[5]

As this person states, there is a tendency not to take risks, so creativity and, indeed, belief become meaningless. Faith, by its very definition, means an assent of trust without certainty. Personal opinions become very narrow and obstinate in order for the priest to maintain this rigid self-protection and avoid being seen as human. New ideas are held in suspicion. There is very little delight in life because of the self-critical enslavement that accompanies this pathology. These priests constantly look for errors, their own and those of others, rather than focus on the potential in people. So, one negative archetypal outcome of this disorder is excessive dogmatism.

What Research Shows

In the research findings, perfectionistic or obsessive-compulsive priests are characterized as apprehensive, fearful, worried, ruminative, excessively organized, persistent, agitated, and rigid. This is accompanied by difficulties in concentrating, problems making decisions, a fear of failure, and generally less productive behavior. The Minnesota Multiphasic Personality Inventory (MMPI) calls this psychasthenia. A person with a high score on this scale is described as having excessive doubts, pressures, preoccupations, and unreasonable fears. This type of priest would be very anxious, tense, and agitated, engaging in excessively ritualistic behavior, and having feelings of insecurity and inferiority.[6]

Surprisingly, a high score on this scale of the MMPI has actually been shown to indicate endurance in the seminary:

Of all the complex indicators of one's ability to persevere in his studies for the priesthood, those dealing with his anxiety and compulsivity seem to be the clearest. Much research, in addition to the one here reported on, bears out this statement.[7]

This finding suggests that there is, indeed, some hopeful archetypal meaning in this disorder. These seminarians persist to ordination. This compulsivity is, therefore, often encouraged as an advantage in the vocation.

The group (seminarians) is characterized by "phobias or compulsive behavior" and by "mild depression, excessive worry, lack of confidence, or inability to concentrate."[8]

Many researchers have verified this perfectionistic, obsessive-compulsive aspect of priesthood,[9] describing priests as rigid, moralistic, right, superior, and good.[10] After a priest leaves the seminary, this compulsive perfectionism can turn into a type of flawless workaholism in which work is used as a substitute for unsatisfied intimacy needs.

What emerged was that, in addition to high achievement orientation, etc., most ... of the religious felt that they heightened their
work commitments and life because they found little or no nour-
ishment from and in their local community ... Essentially, individuals described stress resulting in impaired interpersonal and
social/communal relations which, in turn, gave rise to further
intensification of work as a substitute.[11]

The National Conference of Catholic Bishops' report *The Health of American Catholic Priests* concludes that 66.4% of the priests who responded often or sometimes worry about things. 82.3% say that they often or sometimes have stress in their life and work, and 63.4% state that they are sometimes or often nervous.[12] Those under 35 years of age seem to have reported higher scores in these areas.[13]

The Center for Human Development describes 60% of the priests in its inquiry as workaholic, 48% experiencing tension between identity and behavior, 43% expressing guilt, and 57% having anxiety concerning confrontation. Numerous priests seem to have perfectionistic anxi-
ety about health issues:

Many of the priests do not consider exercise, movement, and paying attention to their bodies to be important parts of the spiritual
life. Nevertheless, many expressed anxiety about physical illness,
weight, and personal appearance. These findings suggest a need
to integrate the physical into their spiritual lives.[14]

It can be theorized here that an inability to integrate the physical is related to a fear of sexuality. Therefore, obsessive-compulsive perfectionism in priests might reflect sexual anxiety.

41% reported at least slight anxiety about their faith and about
changes in the church ... The concern that produces the most anxiety for the priests is in the area of inter-personal relationships;

57% reported much anxiety about confrontations. High on the list of social concerns are anxieties about loneliness and sexuality.[15]

Priests who feel constrained by the institution and by these scrupulous symptoms of sublime holiness are likely to suppress their real feelings and thoughts, leading to passive-aggressive behavior.[16] This is particularly true in relation to sexual acting out, which, in a hierarchical framework where celibacy is demanded, becomes an unconscious means of expressing discontent.[17]

These priests fit a description that David Burns calls "the perfectionist's script for self-defeat," that finds its expression in moralism and dogmatism.[18] Perfectionists are unable to live with ambiguity and ambivalence. Only the extremes of the human behavioral continuum exist in their minds.[19]

Perfectionism leads to lying and secrecy. Because of this, many priests maintain split lives. They try to present a holy, idealized, and perfect image when "on the job," but often have very opposite lives when on vacation or when away from the ministry. A recent study indicates that perfectionism is associated with a tendency to deny personally deviant behavior and to present oneself in the best possible light.[20] This is certainly true for many priests.

Compulsion and Compassion

"The only way a person can be perfect is to be imperfect ..., without imperfections any system becomes stagnant."[21] An obsessive-compulsive disorder affects priests in that they become, over time, quite sluggish and stale when trapped in its negative archetype. The words of Paul to the Corinthian community need to be heeded: "...When I am powerless, it is then that I am strong" (2 Corinthians 12:10). Priests really need the courage to begin practicing imperfection. How, then, do we understand the idea expressed by the Gospel writer: "In a word, you must be made perfect as God in heaven is perfect" (Matthew 5:48)? Commenting on this passage from the Gospel of Matthew, the biblical scholar John L. McKenzie says:

This verse is conflated from Deuteronomy 18:13 and Leviticus 19:2, where the word holy is used. "Perfect" represents the Hebrew word for "whole" or "integral;" it is the love of one's enemies that insures the integrity of Christian morality and distinguishes it from merely ethical morality.[22]

Perfectionistic priests cannot love their enemies, either the shadows within themselves or the enemies outside. Thus, they are not conscientiously embracing their own integrity. In addition, because they flee from any recognition of their own personal imperfections, they find empathy difficult. Compassion is developed when a priest recognizes personal imperfection. A priest cannot "suffer with" another person unless individual weakness has been embraced and endured.

What, then, of the perfection and omnipotence of God? His perfection and omnipotence must include what seems to us the very opposite: His incompleteness, His vulnerability. In which case, Jesus is the very image of divinity in a way that we could hardly dare to think.[23]

The Jungian analyst, Adolf Guggenbuhl-Craig, talks about this in terms of getting in touch with the invalid inside us. "We are all born invalids," he says, "none of us is perfect."[24] This invalid archetype is central to the transformation of priesthood since it counteracts arrogance and allows one to develop humility. If trapped in a perfectionistic, negative archetype, priests will choose power and ego inflation as a compensation to replace the wounded, internal invalid.

A Variety of Signs

The historian of priesthood, Leopold Sabourin, S.J., says that the priestly vocation is seen in a variety of signs. Among these are certain deformities, illnesses, and even insanity.[25] Another historian, E.O. James, commenting on the primal precursors to priesthood, says that "weak and sickly people are often selected for the office ..."[26]

Our blindness to the place and importance of the invalid archetype becomes a moralistic attitude ... It is our failure to accept the invalid in each of us ... that makes us unable to cope with the archetype of the invalid when we meet it (in others).[27]

The author goes on to say that "the figure of the Imperfect can only be seen upon the ground of the Perfect."[28] So, these disordered obsessive-compulsive traits in the priesthood are a clear message that imperfection is being denied. The stronger the need for perfection the greater the need to deny its opposite.

We can only relate in an empathic and responsive way toward others when we have been confronted by our own personal suffering and weakness.[29] True perfection includes compassion. As the Gospel of Luke expresses it, "Be compassionate as God is compassionate" (Luke 6:36). A priest has to recognize personal imperfection in order to be compassionate. Human perfection is imperfection.

As stated earlier, contemporary culture, with its emphasis on co-dependency, can reflect this obsessive-compulsive pathology. The extremes of this movement, which is so popular in current literature and media, create an atmosphere where a person can no longer care for another without being labeled codependent. The priesthood, as an empathetic profession, needs to stand in opposition to this fashionable movement away from compassion.

An Obstacle to Compassion

Compulsion is the primary obstacle to works of compassion. Compulsion, which seeks order, dogma, and excessive independence, causes a priest to depend only on institutionalized moral rigidity. It is often seen as scrupulosity. Recognizing imperfections, on the other hand, can limit these compulsions and bring about a positive response to this archetypal dynamic by enabling greater flexibility.

This is not to say that a priest needs to live outside the institution or resort to rebelliousness. In fact, that would be merely another extreme way of responding. However, there is a great difference between dogmatic priesthood and compassionate priesthood. Dogma seeks orthodoxy while a more benevolent approach seeks and understands paradox. The priesthood, as the gospels imply, needs to have a deeper awareness of "paradoxy" rather than orthodoxy if compassionate ministry is to prosper (cf. Matthew 23 and Luke 11:37 ff).[30]

This perfectionistic compulsion can be understood by relating it to two age-old apostasies in the church. The first is called Pelagianism, which held that the autonomous efforts of people could be exerted until virtue and excellence were achieved. Pelagianism is a type of compulsive striving after holiness. In this belief system, it is always something outside oneself that compels to greater and greater activity, not personal integrity.

On the other hand, priests cannot fall into the trap of Quietism, the opposite heresy, which postulates that people need not engage in any activity because grace will act without any requirement for human responsibility. Perfectionism can lead to both heresies, compulsive superiority or obsessive apathy. Both of these extremes promote irresponsibility in priests.

Love of Enemies

Loving one's enemies, which as McKenzie suggests is associated with the perfection of God, actually implies a lack of human perfection. If we have enemies, we are forced to recognize our differences and multiplicity; in our enemies we are graced with an awareness of imperfection. These enemies exist externally, but also exist within each diverse personality. Priests need to love the enemy within themselves, the shadow of perfectionistic ideals, implicitly understanding that they are powerless and vulnerable in the light of these disorders.

Imperfections can assure a priest that this vocation mediates the multiplicity of the human condition. "We are morally enriched by contrast and diversity."[31] As Samuels adds, through our imperfections we can arrive at "moral imagination ... which ... generates tolerance, forgiveness, openness, and an ingenuous approach to problems."[32] Obsessive-compulsive priests are rarely very creative because they fear making mistakes. They usually have no imagination. So, compulsive moralism replaces compassion.

Priesthood needs to mediate the experience of imperfection because there is no ideal human being and no perfect consistency within a person, relationship, group, or the world. Everyone is in ambiguous process, as is all of creation. God's life exists in everything. So, imperfection is a sign of God's ongoing creation. Perfection is the devious enemy.

Patient Endurance

We strive to present ourselves as ministers of God, acting with patient endurance amid trials, difficulties, distresses, beatings, imprisonments, and riots; as those familiar with hard work, sleepless nights, and fastings; conducting ourselves with innocence, knowledge, and patience ... as people with the message of truth and the power of God ... We are called imposters, yet we are truthful; nobodies who are in fact well known; dead, yet here we are, alive; punished, but not put to death; sorrowful, though we are always rejoicing; poor, yet we enrich many. We seem to have nothing, yet everything is ours! (2 Corinthians 6:4–10)

Paradoxically, compulsion and perfection, even though they are already forms of rigidity, need to become hardened. In this way, they can crack. Through patient endurance, priests can experience the positive outcome of this pattern. The word endurance has its roots in the Latin meaning "hardening" or persistence. It is also associated with concepts like tolerance, acceptance, resignation, composure, and equanimity. These qualities can, indeed, lead a priest beyond obsessive-compulsive perfectionistic responses. To obsess is to be persistently preoccupied. To be compelled is to be forced, to be under constraint.

Priests need to practice patient endurance as a form of atonement. What needs to be endured is not perfectionistic moral dogmatism, but the personal suffering and imperfection that comes from being human—and therefore imperfect. Entering the province of imperfection requires composure, not compulsion; it requires perseverance, not obsession. This patient endurance, which is so necessary for the priesthood today, can open priests to perceive themselves as cracked vessels who mediate the need for of God's grace.

The word "passion" also has its roots in this concept. A person's initiation into imperfection is an excursion into the true meaning of sacrifice. St. John of the Cross, a person who lived this dynamic, was aware of the gifts that can come from suffering humility. He says, describing the dark journey:

Softened and humbled by aridities and hardships and by other temptations and trials in which God exercises the soul in the course of this night, a person becomes meek toward God and himself, and also toward his neighbor. As a result he will no longer become impatiently angry with himself and his faults, nor with his neighbor's, neither is he displeased or disrespectfully querulous with God for not making him perfect quickly.[33]

Here, we are reminded that "contemplation has been replaced by activism" in our society.[34] Obsession and compulsion, in addition to destroying compassion, also hamper contemplation. And this is precisely where one of the major transitions needs to take place. Contemplation, as stated earlier, is essential if priests are ever going to discover the positive message in these "perfectionistic" traits.

The Perfection of Imperfection

Perfectionism is the product of a desire to avoid personal suffering. It has been said that obsessive-compulsive disorder is actually a deep-seated way to deal with a fear of death. We see this in the fields of medicine and psychology, with their compelling need to cure, heal, and avoid death. Jean Vanier, a holy man of our time, who has discovered creativity and grace in developmentally disabled people, writes:

In our times there is a danger of thinking that everyone may become perfectly healed and find perfect unity in themselves and with others. This type of idealism is rampant everywhere. New therapies engender more and better illusions. And each day new techniques are born which will bring about this long-awaited healing. Personally, I am more and more convinced that there is no perfect healing. Each human being carries their own wounds, their own difficulties of relationships and their own anguishes. It is a question of learning to live day after day with this reality and not in a state of illusion ...[35]

Perfection grasps at power. Imperfection embraces limitation and weakness.

The kingdom of God, central as it is to Jesus' message, cannot be understood if one does not also perceive the extent of this kingdom: it included the poor, the "anawim." ... The leaders of the Jewish people, the priests, the scribes, and the pharisees, realized only too clearly that Jesus by associating with such anawim and publicly stating that they belonged to the kingdom was undermining their authority. It was the priests who in many ways declared such people "sinners" and thereby excommunicated them from the "pious Jews." ... When Jesus publicly tells his opponents that these sinners will go to heaven before they do, their authority is being publicly challenged. This is indeed bad news for them ... Only when one catches in the preaching of Jesus both the good news and the bad news will one begin to understand why Jesus ended up being rejected and killed.[36]

In their extreme beliefs, perfectionistic priests can tend toward a total dependence on institutional dogmas while denouncing personal creativity, liberty, and faith. It is precisely here that they end up becoming prejudiced and bigoted. On the other hand, when in the "sinner syndrome," such priests reject all outside input and objectivity. Perfectionism leads them from one extreme to the other.

The Need for Balance

Priests need to live out the balance between these two realities so that they can mediate a synthesis of faith, freedom, and responsibility. There is always a danger that human beings will surrender themselves totally to the "law" (the rule of collective) or entirely to personal opinion. Faith requires a two-way dialectic. It is the obligation of a priest to bear witness to the following truth: surrendering exclusively to one's own desires or surrendering totally to institutional morality are both forms of egotism and arrogance.

The perfectionistic priest will scrupulously allow the institution to control everything in life, while becoming sociopathic in dealings with others, or he will end up deciding everything independently of any collegial input. Both extremes make decisions of conscience almost impossible: in truth, both the individual and the institution are inspired. How, then, can a common-good decision be reached? Of course, the answer to this requires a gamble of faith. Perfectionistic priests refuse to take these risks. They forget that if the gamble fails, we are brought back by forgiveness. If a risk is taken, and it proves to be "wrong," then the archetype of priesthood declares that reconciliation is possible.

Every human venture is imperfect! If everything were perfect we would have no need for God.

By experiencing imperfection, priests are blessed to confront the injustices and prejudices of our time. Being perfectionistic, however, can hold a priest bound to abusive patriarchal power structures. The negative archetypal forces will then become overwhelming and will be expressed in obsessive-compulsive symptoms. Perfectionism leads priests away from relatedness, and when they cannot relate to the sinful, imperfect invalid within themselves, they will surely be unable to relate to and have compassion for the invalid in others. Without empathy and compassion, a priest is likely to participate in psychopathic abuses of power and authority.

CHAPTER FIVE

From Abusive Power to Intimacy

This lack of Eros in psychopaths finds expression in difficulties encountered in interpersonal relationships. Rather than Eros, we frequently find manipulation. Jung said that when Love retreats, Power advances; Power being of signal importance in individuals with psychopathic tendencies. Where Eros is lacking, manipulation, control, domination, and intrigue take over.[1]

As the historian Kenan Osborne states, leadership within the Christian community is the hallmark of priestly ministry in the early church. He goes on to contend that presidency over the community is far more important in the sub-apostolic church than presidency over the eucharist or sacramental ministry. "Ministerial leadership in general is the basis for eucharistic leadership in particular."[2] Leadership, therefore, is a substantial aspect of the priestly vocation.

This belief is substantiated by E.O. James, who explains in his study on the nature and function of priesthood that a priest's role is to promote the welfare of the whole community.[3] The priest always mediates for the community before God. Even in primal societies, the priesthood is associated with authority, specialization, distinction, and leadership.[4]

The Abuses of Priestly Power

History is the first to teach us that leaders can become corrupt and exploit their power. Corruption of leadership in the priesthood has been thoroughly investigated over the past fifty years. It is described as "antisocial personality." The symptoms associated with this disorder are: asocial or antisocial behavior, compulsion, rebelliousness, impulsivity, narcissism, poor judgment, immaturity, superficiality in relationships, and authority conflicts. An antisocial personality creates a good first impression without the ability to maintain protracted relationships. Fleeting involvements are often the norm, as opposed to long-term intimacy.

Many researchers have commented on antisocial personality in relationship to priesthood. In a 1948 pioneering study, W.C. Bier investigated 171 Catholic seminarians and compared their Minnesota Multiphasic Personality Inventory (MMPI) scores with those of medical, dental, law, and undergraduate college students. Bier discovered that seminarians scored higher on the psychopathic deviance scale than these other professionals. He was so upset by these conclusions that he determined many of the items in the MMPI ought not to apply to seminarians. He tried to explain why such aberrant scores appeared in their testing. "In the mind of this writer," Bier stated, "this leads to the conclusion that the MMPI will function more effectively as a diagnostically useful instrument in testing the adjustment of seminarians if certain items are eliminated."[5] In 1956, Bier revised the MMPI for use with seminarians, stating that "the seminary is a distinctly more special group than would usually be encountered."[6]

In 1962, Charles Weisgerber used Bier's adaptations of the MMPI in his analysis of 211 candidates studying for the priesthood. The femininity scale was highest in 50% of the profiles (meaning that seminarians showed stereotypically "feminine" traits). The next most frequent type, even after using Bier's adapted test, had high scores on the psychopathic deviance scale, or antisocial personality. Weisgerber, too, was startled by these findings and said:

> This is puzzling in a group of men who have chosen a life of obedience. Perhaps the scale reflects a certain amount of independence, which may be healthy or unhealthy.[7]

Weisgerber's colleague, Petreolus Hispanicus, writing in this same book, entitled *Screening Candidates for the Priesthood and Religious Life*, defines this MMPI scale as follows:

> The psychopathic deviate ... is one with apathy of emotional life. This connotes the fact that he lacks emotional responses suitable to a given situation, as well as the fact that he does not show emotions at all in situations in which one would normally expect him to do so.[8]

Another researcher, Ralph Dunn, criticized Bier's attempted justifications. He said: "When Bier tested his revised form with seminarians, he found that they obtained even higher scores on his modified form."[9] Dunn concludes:

> The difficulty with Bier's reasoning at this point is that he seems to make the assumption that the seminary group is well adjusted. Subsequent researchers have found it necessary to test this hypothesis.[10]

Studies have found seminarians engaging in self-aggrandizement, and conclude that this is a reason why they score so high in psychopathic deviance. In other words, these men faked answers to many questions because they were trying to appear to be psychologically healthy when they took the test. This is where the secrecy and repression are so noticeable. When the seminarians lied in answering certain questions, they scored higher on the antisocial personality scale.[11] This is a reflection of the idealization that was mentioned earlier as a feature of perfectionism.

These seminarians desperately wanted to be impeccable and exemplary. Obviously, this stems from trying to fulfill strong external expectations. Eventually, these expectations become internalized, repressed, held in secret, and they are transformed into antisocial traits. So these priests actually develop what they have tried to avoid, and are not perfect at all. They become what they hate.

In another study, Weisgerber again expressed his incredulity concerning the number of seminarians who were high in psychopathic deviance:

> It has been something of a mystery to the writer why psychopathic deviance, which presumably indicates a tendency to show the characteristics of the classical psychopathic personality, should run high on the average and be so frequently the highest score in a group of seminarians.[12]

He finally concludes that "the scale is valid all along the line ... The implication, then, would be that a sizeable proportion of the seminarians have at least a tendency in common with the psychopathic deviate."[13]

In a similar study done on priests who had lived for fourteen years or more in a religious order, it was discovered that they had a higher than usual degree of depression.

> [They also showed an] absence of deep emotional response ... Consequently, the only prudent statement that can be made about the data ... in a qualitative sense is that the experimental group of this thesis performs in ways somewhat similar to the ways in which paranoid, effeminate (or highly cultured), hysteric, and asocial psychopathic personalities perform.[14]

These findings were even stronger than those of the previous research. After studying hospitalized priests, two psychologists observed the following: "Religious patients outnumbered lay patients two to one in personality disorders. Clergy patients were particularly high in incidence of sociopathic personality."[15] (The terms sociopathic personality or antisocial personality are other expressions for psychopathic deviance.) This same article found that sexual acting out was a behavior associated with antisocial personality. This corresponds to the association made in the previous chapter concerning sexual expression and passive-aggressive behavior in priests.

> We were impressed in this regard by Harry Stack Sullivan's description of the sociopath as one who sought "fugitive, fleeting involvements with other people." Perhaps this is the role in which the Catholic clergymen are able to function best—living out some of these fugitive, fleeting involvements because of the rather transient lives they sometimes lead, not only in frequent changes of post, but also in the impermanence of many of their meaningful relationships.[16]

Antisocial Personality Traits

Many other investigators have commented on the incidence of antisocial personality traits in seminarians and priests who score high on dominance and also high on inferiority scales.[17] This could certainly suggest tendencies that are in keeping with this disorder. The Center for Human Development, in its recent study of priests in the United States, concludes that they are angry, belligerent, and have poor relationships. In this analysis, 52% of the priests tended to view people negatively (p. 13) and 68% were predisposed toward prejudiced judgments (p. 14).[18]

Other studies, too, have found clergymen to be hostile, distant, and having authority problems.[19] In their sociological study, Andrew Greeley and his associates contend that priests have problems with authority.[20] The same was reported by Douglas Hall in his probe into the work-lives of priests:

> We conclude that authority is the central explanatory concept in understanding the amount of psychological success the priest experiences. This conclusion is based on the fact that priests, especially curates, are almost unable to describe any aspect of their careers without considering authority.[21]

Luigi M. Rulla, a Jesuit psychologist, in two studies of seminarians, found them to have problems with dominance and aggression. He also discovered that Catholic seminarians were rebellious and narcissistic. Father Rulla suggests that antisocial tendencies might be produced by subconscious, underlying, and unresolved personal conflicts in priests.[22]

Other authors[23] make reference to clergy having authority problems and antisocial tendencies.

> Because of their extreme self-centeredness, they tended to be opportunistic and self-seeking, caring little about the feelings and opinions of others. Thus they tended to exploit others for their own sensual satisfactions and used their office to this end. Along with this behavior they had a marked ability to rationalize their behavior. To the uncritical observer, they might have appeared to be misunderstood until experience demonstrated how mistaken the observer was.[24]

Misused Power and Authority

This disorder, then, can actually be understood as a condition of misused power and authority, which can often be covered up with external shows of piety. These symptoms point directly to the quality of today's priestly leadership, which may be losing its credibility.

Priestly leadership is being denounced today by those within and outside the church, people in parishes, hierarchical authorities, the modern media, and even priests themselves. It seems that there must be some reason for this, beyond the rationalization of "democratic tendencies" in the church. This criticism reflects the antisocial (psychopathic) characteristics that we have examined.

This same critique, however, may be the source for transforming priestly leadership. The word "psychopath" actually comes from the Greek meaning suffering (*pathos*) of soul (*psyche*). By being in touch with the personal suffering that the abusive use of power and excessive authority causes, a priest can be led to a positive archetypal expression in benevolent leadership. Without this awareness, however, negative power advances in the place of love. A priest will merely imitate the abusive power that has caused this suffering and will inflict it on others as well.

Celibacy and Power

Celibacy, in reality, has very little to do with sex and sexuality. For thousands of years, we in Western societies have successfully projected our repressed and ugly desires onto sexuality. In truth, celibacy has more to do with power and dominance than it does with sex. I was reminded of this just yesterday when I heard a news story about a male prisoner in Texas who wants to be castrated so that he will no longer impulsively molest children. People in the medical profession are leery of this because they say that there is no scientific evidence that castration will prevent someone from molesting other people. This is so because that act is not primarily sexual; it has to do with violence and power.

Celibacy must been seen in the context of power as well. Sex and sexuality are wonderful gifts with which God has blessed the created world. The church, and Western society in general, needs to stop using sex as a scapegoat for all of our other difficulties.

In light of this, I want to suggest that the discipline of celibacy can amplify the disorder of antisocial personality in priestly leadership. As the word celibacy implies, this pathology is associated with being asocial. To be social is to ally oneself with another; it involves sexual (though not necessarily genital) rapport and companionship. Being asocial can become an undesirable by-product of enforced celibacy, since this regimen has, both directly and indirectly, forbidden close and intimate associations with other human beings. Priests who have close relationships are usually held in suspicion. However, priests who are isolated and feel inferior will necessarily resort to activities focused on getting more power.

In point of fact, to be an authentic leader, a priest needs companionship; a priest needs to experience the realities of relating closely to another human being. True leadership comes from such an encounter. How can a priest guide and lead others through the territory of love and interpersonal connection when this domain is not personally experienced?

Celibacy is directly related to authority problems. Kenneth Mitchell, a psychologist at the Menninger Foundation, in a psychological analysis of celibacy, states that "celibates will have authority hangups."[25] Robert McAllister, who studied mental illnesses in clergy, maintained the belief that sexual acting out among celibate priests was related to authority problems.[26] Mitchell describes a state of "perpetual adolescence" which tends to be maintained in priests through the discipline of mandatory celibacy. As with adolescents, then, sexual acting out can become a defensive way to express frustration with authority figures (parental images).[27] Celibacy as a discipline becomes management by guilt. A very good analysis of this can be found in a book by Michael Crosby called *Celibacy: Means of Control or Mandate of the Heart.*[28]

Recognized by the Bishops

This phenomenon has also been recognized by the U.S. Catholic Bishops in their investigation of low morale in the priesthood.[29] Daniel Nelson, citing this study on morale, states:

> This document identifies the lack of openness by church administration to discuss optional celibacy in the context of changing understandings of sexuality and sexual orientation as a major contributing factor to the current low morale among Catholic clergy. It identified this rigidity towards mandatory celibacy as a major reason a) for leaving the priesthood, b) for the shortage of vocations, and c) for loneliness and personal unhappiness of those who stay.[30]

More than twenty years ago, Robert Loftus, in his Ph.D. dissertation, concluded: "Celibacy, because it is a grace from God, cannot be legislated for an entire group without risking the exposure of a good number of individuals to serious psychological problems."[31] Crosby, in an earlier work titled *The Dysfunctional Church,* says that it is difficult enough to live a celibate life that is understood as a charism:

> It is another thing to have it imposed by a hierarchy that can afford to be asexual because its identity does not come from relationships that are intimate and generative but rather from power and patriarchy.[32]

Antisocial characteristics can surface in their negative manifestation because of enforced celibacy. Struggles with dependence and independence come to the fore, in which priests attempt to control their lives and ministries while at the same time being totally dependent upon the institution.

This split can create a style of leadership that ignores input from other people, because these priests do not have faith in others. "The lack of trust in anyone is the main stumbling block with sociopaths. Sociopaths don't trust anyone; they suspect everybody."[33] These priests have very little sense of mutuality and interdependence. So, in their fear of establishing closer relationships, their mediocre faith can be expressed in secrecy, lying, and abusive power, the negative expression of archetypal leadership.

I believe that enforced celibacy can encourage the emergence of an authoritarian style in which decisions are made and merely announced. This happens because a priest has no experience working intimately with others and is not sensitive to the give and take of attachment, conflict, and loss. Such a priest is not able to consult people or enable others in their ministerial roles. Priestly authority becomes compulsive, driven, impulsive, without contemplation and compassion. Rebelliousness can become a way of relating, both in relationship to those in authority over the priest and in associations with parishioners or those to whom the priest is considered a leader.

Signs of Rebellion

Acting out in a sexual manner is one of the primary manifestations of this rebelliousness. For many priests there is no better way to get the attention of a bishop or superior than by getting caught doing something sexual. Enforced celibacy and antisocial behavior are linked in the priesthood. The symptoms of antisocial behavior include apathy of emotion, self-aggrandizement, exploitation, and superficiality. Enforced celibacy has encouraged this type of apathy, in which priests can end up having only elusive and fleeting involvements with other people.

Narcissism is also related to this disorder. This is a name that comes from the familiar Greek myth of Narcissus. The flower which was left at the end of that tale had sedative properties (*Narkissos*). Our word narcotic comes from this root. A narcotic drug produces a type of torpor in those who take it. Enforced celibacy can be related to this deadening of emotions which is similar to the effects of using chemicals.

Also, any passion for life can be squelched by this sedation.

The incidence of alcoholism among priests is significant here because antisocial personality disorders are often connected to chemical dependency.[34] The drug medicates against isolation and loneliness and the anxiety that is experienced about relationships. In the end, though, alcohol and drugs only lead to greater isolation. These are common disorders in the priesthood and indicate that a priest has become alienated, unfriendly, antagonistic, cynical, hostile. Emotions become passive;[35] lethargy and isolation set in. Relationships remain impermanent and transitory.

This narcissistic numbness of emotion is a form of immaturity and reveals a lack of intimacy. Priests do not develop psychologically, spiritually, or emotionally when they have not freely chosen celibacy. They become quite superficial, concerned mostly with external devotion; troubled or enamored by looks and appearances; obsessed with their image and how they come across to superiors and those whom they serve.

Seminary training can promote this superficiality by encouraging outward demonstrations of piety as a substitute for passionate living. As Morton Kelsey explains in reference to this phenomenon of shallow piety:

> The role of the priest is most essential in society. Unless he regains his position in the very heart and center of society, I question whether this civilization of ours can hold together and not collapse. The priest is the one who is, or should be, mediator of a vast realm of reality which relates to the spirit of things, rather than to the outer physical world ...[36]

To be in touch with this "vast realm of society," a priest must necessarily develop enthusiasm, zest, and fervor for life. Celibacy, when it is freely chosen, certainly has a place within the archetypal priesthood. When celibacy is enforced and not freely chosen, however, it may cause the very immaturity and paralysis that prevents priests from engagement in life. Priests, if they choose to function within the institutional hierarchy, must take personal responsibility for choosing celibacy. Otherwise, they continue to relinquish their power and become resentful.

Cooperation Verses Competition

The natural world has an elaborate system of checks and balances. I want to propose that one of these may be celibacy. First of all, celibacy can serve as a check for unmitigated dominance on the part of human males. Male dominance is associated, in the animal world (of which we are a part), with sexuality and competition for a mate. Elective celibacy can offer a male the opportunity to choose cooperation rather than competition. This has been recognized in many human societies, and also in the world of primates.

Cooperation can be encouraged by celibacy. In nature, the phenomenon of competition comes from males trying to dominate one another in order to get the finest mate (one who can produce the most and "best" offspring and, therefore, generate his genes). Also, this dominance and competition mean that the male may take more than one mate in order to achieve this purpose. Males do not necessarily stop the competition once they have found a suitable mate (cf. the 50% divorce rate in this country). Males tend to keep up the dominant displays in order to find younger, healthier, and more attractive mates.

Celibates, however, if they freely choose this way of life, do not need to be concerned with this competition. Also, in some cultures celibacy is often chosen after offspring have been reproduced.[37] If celibacy is imposed, it might actually feed the psychopathic deviance by causing a regression of instinctual needs and desires, which can only erupt in dominating displays if they find no outlet in intimate altruism and cooperation. Priests need to be honest with themselves and ask whether or not their celibate commitment stems from a fear of sex or intimacy. If so, such fear is often expressed in the abuses of power. Repression of sexual impulses and desires only creates a monster, and enforced celibacy is a form of this subjugation.

Competition has spread to other areas of life as well. For example, people seek dominating control in business, economics, politics, and sports. Having satisfied the need for a partner, then, does not necessarily insure the discharge of this power, just as participation in competitive sporting events is not necessarily an answer to the maintenance of celibacy in seminaries.

Priesthood Encourages Competition

Hierarchical institutions such as the priesthood tend to encourage competition: one attempts to be more central than another, competing for a higher position (pastor, monsignor, bishop, archbishop). This cutthroat and dog-eat-dog structure is certainly not helpful in terms of living out a celibate life. In fact, it is highly counterproductive to celibacy.

Celibacy has the potential to enhance priestly cooperation. When priests no longer need to compete with one another (and now with lay ministers as well), a collegial form of leadership can emerge that is characterized by discernment, patience, kindness, compassion, caring, and understanding.

Cooperation with those in authority also enters into this hypothesis. Do priests feel that they have the collaboration of other members in the hierarchy, especially those in authority over them, or are they treated as inferior males in a system where authority figures frown upon personal autonomy and responsibility? If this is the case, immaturity will be fostered. Priests need to have some sense of control over their own lives if celibacy is ever going to become a viable choice. Otherwise, the immaturity is bound to result in sexual problems or other pathologies.

The responsibility for this promise of celibacy needs to be taken in a cooperative manner. The priests making the promise, along with those who represent the church, are entering into a contract similar to marriage. They are responsible to one another. Celibacy cannot be an individualistic endeavor. It needs cooperation, collegiality, and common trust if it is to be lived out in integrity. Celibacy cannot be lived in isolation.

The essential qualities of priesthood relate to cooperation and mediation, not dominance and competition. When celibacy is enforced, it leads to a repression of emotions and passions, further inflaming the need for dominance and abusive power. In light of this, involuntary celibacy, rather than being a benefit, becomes contrary to the mediatory function of priesthood because it takes away freedom and responsibility by using power to compel a response.

When celibacy is not freely chosen, all of the antisocial symptoms that accompany interpersonal superficiality and lack of mature development arise: authority conflicts, sexual acting out, rebelliousness, impulsiveness, poor judgment, manipulation of others, and rationalization of behavior. These are obviously not appropriate expressions of priestly leadership.

Qualifications for Leadership

In a document prepared by The Center for Human Development as a precursor to the 1990 Synod of International Bishops on the formation of priests, the following recommendations were made concerning priestly leadership:

> For a priest to be a servant-leader, embodying the gospel message of reconciliation and freedom in his personhood and in his relationships with others, he must be emotionally mature, competent in a variety of areas, and able to engage people on a deeply personal level. Mediating the "good news" through personal presence and dialogue demands the following abilities: to reflect upon one's self and one's interior state; to accept one's self with both strengths and weaknesses; to trust in the basic goodness of one's body and emotions; to integrate these and use them in relating to other persons; to allow others to be themselves; to transcend the images and stereotypes that ordinarily interfere with genuine encounter; and to practice existential humor, which manifests itself only at the higher stages of development.[38]

Theologian Karl Schelkle states that the New Testament community was very suspicious of the priestly state as it had been handed down from the Scribes and Pharisees.[39] In fact, the word priest (*hiereus*) was not used because of the power and prestige with which it was associated. In the primitive church, priestly power was very suspect; collegiality was the primary form of leadership. However, as the church became more and more aligned with the power of the Roman Empire and took on many of the trappings of this oligarchy, the priesthood became a separate and isolated authority structure. Schelkle also maintains that the Reformation and Counter-Reformation led to an even further diminishment of the communal aspect of priestly authority.

> And so the official authorities in the Old Church and their theologians saw themselves forced to concentrate so heavily on the

then traditional doctrine of the special priesthood that Catholic teaching and practice became frankly one-sided. The biblical and then traditional Catholic doctrine of the universal priesthood remained valid in principle but was pushed into the background by the strong emphasis on the special priesthood; it became obscure and practically forgotten.[40]

This priesthood of distinction reached its apex in the church at the First Vatican Council.

Priesthood of Believers

Ever since the documents of the Second Vatican Council were promulgated, the church has been attempting to counteract that inclination. In fact, the first paragraph of the Decree on the Ministry and Life of Priests emphasizes the priesthood of all believers. This document describes the functions of ordained priestly leadership: 1) preaching and sharing the gospel of truth, 2) the work of sanctification, and 3) shepherding the people of God in their various vocations within the Christian community.[41] The Council documents refer here to the classic description, which was explained earlier in this book, concerning the prophetic, sacrificial, and messianic roles which the priest is called upon to take.

The next section of this document beautifully describes the necessity for priests to be connected to others. Relationships are seen as being central to the proper functioning of the priestly role.[42] Therefore, it seems conclusive that celibacy should not be used as a means of avoiding close, passionate involvement with others.

A repressed priest who has not resolved the issues of sexuality and intimacy will revert to authoritarianism and inflexibility. Isolation, lethargy, excessive control, irritability, and overly controlled attitudes will ultimately be expressed in abuses of power. As the archetypal psychologist James Hillman describes it, the soul begins to "contain its psychopathic potentials."

The Power Shadow

The archetypal shadow side of priestly leadership can also give some important clues to the needs and desires of priesthood that are being neglected. "The dark side of this noble image of the man of God is the lying hypocrite, the man who preaches not because he believes but in order to gain influence and power."[43] This is called a "power shadow." The symptoms of this "power shadow" are similar to those of antisocial personality: asocial, rebellious, impulsive, narcissistic, self-aggrandizing, poor judgment, immature, superficial, authority conflicts, apathy of emotion, exploitive, separate, detached, and aloof.

Excessive dogmatism is associated with this negative archetypal expression. The Jungian analyst Adolph Guggenbuhl-Craig says, "moralists are often not loving ..." Antisocial priests can enter into a state of compensation in which the weaker the sense of love, the greater the moral need. Priests then become morally rigid and compulsively proper.

> These are the people who are always talking about "the principle of the matter." They get so lost in principles that they never notice the need for a little milk of human kindness by way of balance. Compensated psychopaths tend to seek out occupations where those with whom they work will help to maintain a moral rigidity, occupations where a strict morality is the order of the day.[44]

The author goes on to list the priesthood as one of these professions. In reality, such compensation can be an attempt to shore up a priest's own weak morality and absent sense of relational connectedness.

A Search for Power and Control

Curiously, unconscious feelings of victimization and sexual inadequacy, both of which can be associated with enforced celibacy, may lead to a search for power and abusive control in relationships. Power can be defined as an ability to influence another's behavior. It is aligned with leadership. Both dominance and submission are unfortunate ways in which this power can be achieved. The question is how does a priest choose to have an impact on others?

A priest has certain resources that can be utilized in leadership. First, there are many personal resources, those that depend upon alliances and roles, liking and approval. Personal resources can be attained by either dominant or submissive means (e.g. a dominant means would be to give approval for a job well done; a submissive means would be to deny affection or approval to someone). A priest can easily manipulate others by enforcing the "priestly role." Secondly, there are concrete resources that can be exercised in a leadership capacity. These are related to such things as knowledge, money, and physical strength. An example of this would be for a priest to utilize knowledge of theology in order to manipulate responses from others.

Dominant and submissive forms of power are not always clearly distinguishable in priestly leadership. Dominance can range from brute force to very subtle and passive forms of manipulation. Direct dominance is demonstrated when a priest exerts influence openly, by giving an order or making a request. Submissive dominance is exercised when the influencer obtains the outcome while trying to keep the other person unaware of the control. This is called submissive seduction.

When priests have a certain abhorrence to direct aggressive or assertive pursuits of power, they often engage in these more subtle displays of authority. For example, timidity and helplessness can be very influential in priestly leadership because people can be manipulated into feeling sorry for a priest. And, because the hierarchical structures of priesthood frown upon being directly domineering, these indirect models of submissive dominance tend to prevail.

Sanctioned by Celibacy

These patterns of submissive dominance are sanctioned by enforced celibacy. This is how a scenario might develop. Feeling sexually inadequate, a candidate for priesthood might think that celibacy will resolve this problem. Along with the sexual inadequacy, this person might also be harboring unconscious beliefs associated with low status and poor self-esteem. Feeling inadequate and living in a hierarchical structure causes one to conceal these inner beliefs or hide them with "submissive piety." These beliefs usually center around the irrational thinking that one will inevitably "lose" in adult relationship struggles involving reciprocity. A competitive dynamic is at work. The hierarchical structure serves to increase the unconscious feelings of inadequacy around sexuality because any sexual feelings or actions will be punished. As a result, after this person is ordained, sex or sexual "playing" with someone who appears to be weaker might become a way for this inadequate priest to reduce stress and gain some measure of self-assurance and strength, along with feelings of power, control, and potency. An example of this is when priests become sexually involved with children or others who seem powerless.

Priests sometimes become involved sexually with someone who is more dominant as well, which seems to soothe the unconscious feelings of inferiority, submissiveness, and low self-esteem. Many priests who feel this way tend to relate to their bishops and superiors in this way. All relationships have some sexual component to them.

So, sexual involvement with someone who is perceived as weaker often stems from feelings of sexual deficiency, and sexual involvement with someone who is more dominant can also stem from feelings of sexual inadequacy. Priests often play out this unconscious contradictory dynamic. In order to cope with it, they can submit to enforced celibacy. Because of the hierarchical nature of priesthood, human relationships can then become contests involving "winners" and "losers."

The Victim/Martyr Role

All of this becomes important for the priesthood because of the "victim/martyr" role that is often associated with it. This, too, can be related to sexuality. There are certain erotic gratifications that come from being a martyr. For example, a priest might unconsciously say, when feeling sexually inferior, "contrast my saintliness to those who hurt me," or, "at least God loves me, even if you don't." In this way, the victim becomes the victor; the loser becomes the winner through deception. There is an identification with the Divine Victim. Enforced celibacy is often viewed by priests in this negative framework of "giving up" sex. With this conviction, however, a priest will end up engaging in abuses of power and control, because it is based on feelings of sexual inferiority. This view is enhanced by the messages that priests receive from the patriarchal structures, through which they are discouraged from becoming intimately involved with companions.

Celibacy can also be related to male dominance because it implies that the priest can stand independently on his own two feet. A real man is not "tied down" (listen to the dominant/submissive theme in this phrase). A real man is free. Enforced celibacy has been associated with this "freedom," which supposedly allows priests to devote more time to ministry and interact with more people.

Many priests tend to be rather passive and dependent which implies an interior attitude of submission. Therefore, we can readily see the "set up" for all of the dynamics that have been mentioned above in relationship to priestly power and sexuality. Priests submit to power over them and are dominant in their expression to those "beneath" them.

Intimacy and Humanity

How can this puzzle of dominance and submission be resolved? What does the priesthood need when the negative aspects of power begin to emerge? Perhaps a deeper understanding of these opposing symptoms can give us some idea of how to balance priestly leadership when it is caught in this "power shadow."

In order to accept this psychopathology, a priest needs to recognize that this is an entrance into a labyrinth. When a priest moves away from the isolation of enforced celibacy, panic can ensue, especially if the priest has never experienced intimacy. Many priests, over the years, have gone into therapy in order to deal with the anxiety associated with panic attacks. This is almost always connected to sexuality. So, celibacy may be challenged as a priest becomes closer to another human being. In the process, however, the true archetypal nature can come to the fore.

All too often, though, priests hold these intimate feelings inside. The primary emotion resulting from this can be shame.

> The experience of shame is connected with the experience of earth, and perhaps is a way that may even lead one to the experience of earth ... And so, shame points to something beyond the will—something of power beyond the human, which we might call the divine.[45]

If intimacy is not embraced (and I am not necessarily talking here about genital intimacy), then a priest will not work through the antisocial aspects of this archetype. Being ashamed that one can fall in love removes one from the depths of humanity and may prevent a deeper experience of God.

Friendship, love, intimacy, and passion of emotion can encourage a priest to be genial, gregarious, hospitable, courteous, cordial, gracious, and amiable in his leadership. Feelings of the heart can be enhanced. If an authentic relationship, in other words, one that is based upon mutuality and not dominant/submissive power, is present, then the negative symptoms will subside. A priest will no longer be isolated, estranged, and disengaged in life and leadership styles. Indifference can be replaced by concern, while arrogance and unapproachableness will be displaced by reconciliation and inclusion. A celibate person, one who freely chooses the discipline, can engage in this type of intimacy. If celibacy is enforced, however, it will often facilitate the emergence of the "power shadow."

A priest I have known for fifteen years recently decided to leave the active ministry. I asked him why. He told me that he had a close friend with whom he had had a long-standing relationship. It was a good and healthy relationship. The other members of the community did not like the idea that this priest had a close friend and that he spent time with her. They rejected his friend. He said that he very much wanted to remain a priest and engage in priestly ministry. However, he was simply sick and tired of the jealousy, the politics, and the power games. He was also weary of being treated like a child. He left the active priesthood.

This story is an example of the abuses of authority that can result from this tension between love and power. The members of my friend's community had developed abusive power and control in compensation for their own lack of intimacy. They were not hospitable, social, courteous, or gracious. Their relationships were not based on reciprocity, but on antagonism and alienation, dominance, and submission.

All priests need relationships that are lasting. Passing and transitory friends only make for greater abuses of power. Loving relationships need to be abiding, enduring, and durable. Certainly, this raises the question of whether or not priests should be reassigned so often.

The "power shadow" can be offset by the ardor of emotion rather than apathy of passion. Intimate relationships can instill within a priest an enthusiasm and vigor for life and ministry. The antisocial shadow of enforced, celibate power, which is summarily destroying the priesthood, desperately needs to be balanced by intimacy and relational love. Emphasis, here, is on the word "enforced." As stated earlier celibacy that is freely chosen is not necessarily going to be expressed in this "power shadow." Intimacy is essential in the life of a priest because it enables him to enter into the complexities and the reciprocity of a relationship where dominant/submissive forces are resolved through mutual interaction.

Positive Aggression

Paradoxically, one of the first signs that priestly power is being transformed into loving leadership is aggression. As a priest becomes less apathetic and more assertive, his leadership and life will take on added meaning. Aggression is one of the characteristics of antisocial personality that can be of service to a positive resolution of this archetypal pattern.

Aggression comes from the Latin word *aggredi*, meaning "to approach." "Aggressive fantasy may want to make contact, get in touch, relate. For some, mainly men perhaps, it may be the only way to relate."[46] As sexual inferiority diminishes and intimacy advances in the life of a priest, assertion, proclamation, and announcement of the good news will become a basis for leadership, rather than passive-aggressive power ploys. A priest needs to take control and responsibility for choosing celibacy, rather than seeing it as a discipline being enforced by external authority. This requires a certain amount of aggression. Celibate intimacy is a risk that needs to be taken in freedom. In addition, a priest needs to assert individual rights toward those who are suspicious and/or jealous of the intimate relationships. With the development of this personal responsibility, leadership can become strong and convincing rather than indifferent and dispassionate.

Intimate companionship can also give a priest an experience of true discernment. People who love one another and relate closely always need to make mutual decisions; through disagreements and conflict they learn to negotiate and discern. Priests have very little practice in this area and therefore have a greater tendency to make poor decisions. Their capacity for deduction, good judgment, accurate discrimination, and interpretation is faulty because of this inadequacy.

As was explained in the chapter on perfectionism, without intimate companionship there is greater likelihood that a priest will become compulsive, acting in fanatical and obsessive ways. So, the lack of intimacy can lead to authority conflicts. Priests who live in isolation have a greater propensity for becoming rebellious, defiant, and resistant to those who are in government over them. Intimacy provides an experience of loyalty, which can be carried over into work and relationships with superiors. As a priest freely chooses to move toward relating, greater honesty and openness with authority figures will result. Trust will increase. There will no longer be a childish fear of being punished or rejected when speaking one's mind. Personal responsibility on the part of a priest will lessen authority problems. Add to this the fact that a close relationship requires energy and time. With such intimacy, priests are less likely to spend the majority of time obsessing about relationships with those in authority, who are the central characters in their lives. As stated earlier, most priests can hardly remove themselves from some form of dependency on their superior or bishop. Naturally authority problems will arise, as in adolescence when there is both love and hatred for the parents, wanting to remain bound to them and at the same time wanting to be free. There is no adult mutuality or collegiality.

Finally, priests do not experience healthy human development when they have antisocial and isolated lifestyles. A document on psychological investigations into Catholic priesthood, which was prepared twenty years ago for the U.S. Bishops, stated that the majority of priests were basically underdeveloped.[47] This immaturity is very much related to being asocial and is reflected in inadequate leadership skills. As we have seen, underdeveloped leadership can be manipulative and superficial, based on dominant/submissive patterns.

This immaturity, of course, can be transformed into an awareness of a wider, cosmic call to leadership. A priest who has an intimate relationship certainly will be better able to promote the order of harmony, accepting the diversity and ambiguity that reflect a cosmic consciousness. This is authentic leadership, one that announces the word of truth authoritatively because connection, association, hospitality, compassion, and flexibility are at the core, stemming from a personal experience of intimacy. This is the plan of God, for "it is not good for humans to be alone" (Genesis 2:18).

CHAPTER SIX

From Stereotypes to Role Flexibility

By accepting the feminine, by doing more than observing her plight from the height of our intellectual note-taking and head-shaking, and by recognizing that the physiological qualities we have deemed inferior are actually projections of our own psychological inferiority, we can restore our path to the androgyne.[1]

The issues surrounding gender identity and gender roles are a source of much debate among social scientists.[2] Suffice it to say that "gender identity" basically means that we are self-identified as either male or female. Regarding gender roles in our society, women are stereotypically understood to have qualities associated with "niceness-nurturance" and are described as "socially sensitive, friendly, and concerned with others' welfare, whereas men are expected to manifest behaviors that can be described as dominant, controlling, and independent."[3] Of course, this summarizes culturally conditioned and chauvinistic attitudes toward these characteristics.

Up until a few years ago, men in our culture who exhibited "feminine" qualities were formally understood as having a disorder or pathology associated with homosexuality. This is no longer the case, however, due to improved scientific information that has changed our society's attitudes toward homosexualities, heterosexualities, masculinity, and femininity. Contemporary research suggests that qualities in men such as sociability, sensitivity, tolerance, passivity, submission, peaceloving, and a tendency to make concessions in the face of confrontation have very little to do with homosexualities or gender identity (being a man or a woman).[4] However, many people still maintain mistaken beliefs and prejudices in this regard. The Roman Catholic church, for example, still judges that homosexuality is an inherent disorder.

A great deal of research on the psychological profiles of priests suggests a certain function of passivity and "femininity" in their lives and ministries. This is an archetypal pattern and is called androgyny. Sex educators Masters and Johnson define androgyny as "the combined presence of stereotyped feminine and masculine characteristics in one person."[5] It stems from two Greek words, *andio* meaning male and *gyn* meaning female.

What Research Shows

Priests are often characterized in research literature as being androgynous. Almost every psychological study done on seminarians or on priests[6] indicates that they generally have aesthetic interests, are unassertive, dislike violence, are malleable when it comes to gender roles, are sensitive, creative, passive, compliant, adaptable, and have a high need for abasement (i.e. want to give in and avoid a conflict).[7]

Seminarians are generally higher in these "feminine" traits than men in the general population.[8]

The feminine aspects of the vocation are well supported. Bier (1948) and a number of his students have found that Catholic seminarians score highest on the femininity scale of the MMPI.[9]

Barry and Bordin also found that these seminarians felt insecure and inferior. This insecurity seemed to be partly due to the anxiety of trying to live out these "feminine" traits in a masculinized and patriarchal culture.[10] "Male religious ... tend to have interests and proclivities which are typically feminine, submissive, and dependent."[11]

Other researchers confirm these findings.[12] For example, Frank Kobler, who investigated screening tests for applicants to the religious life, found that his sample of 323 minor seminarians "had profiles that resembled those for females in the general population."[13] The document from the National Conference of Catholic Bishops, *Reflections on the Morale of Priests*, says:

> priests are often, by temperament and personality, anxious to establish harmony and to please. By theology and vocation they are concerned to be healers, reconcilers and builders of the community. These characteristics make tension and outright hostility all the more disheartening and difficult to bear.[14]

This, I suggest, goes to the very core of the androgynous archetype.[15] James Dittes suggests that this high femininity score correlates with altruism.[16] Clergymen are generally dependent, passive-receptive, insecure, conforming, and have a high need for nurturance. In addition, those who are more submissive usually remain in the seminary and are eventually ordained.[17] Dittes concluded that high femininity scores seemed to be a clergy trademark.

Gordon Thomas, in his book concerning celibacy and the church, gives a good summary of this phenomenon:

> Solid psychological evidence now supports an old suspicion: boys and young men with a feminine perception of themselves tended to be attracted to a vocation, and the long years of religious formation often reinforce this pattern. One survey of priests in 1984 revealed that only two out of every ten priests actually saw themselves as masculine, while four out of ten admitted to a strong feminine identification. Father Jamie Filella, a Jesuit professor of psychology, concluded from his own findings in the matter that, on a global scale, only approximately half as many

priests see themselves as masculine as compared with those who view themselves as feminine. This could mean that close to a quarter of a million Catholic clergy have clinically defined feminine-type personalities.[18]

This femininity, he says, can also have a shadow side because a priest can attempt to compensate for it, in a strongly patriarchal church culture, by abusing power. We see again the emergence of the "power shadow" and the conflict between love and power. "It ... is possible for an androgynous individual to combine negative elements of masculinity and femininity such as being domineering and nagging, or being harsh or weak."[19]

A Response to Authority

Seminarians and priests are conditioned to take on "feminine" characteristics in Roman Catholicism as a response to hierarchical authority. Ironically, at the same time, the prevailing patriarchal power does not permit priests to consciously embrace these very same qualities! In this dynamic, women are also rejected.

"Misogyny and heroic masculinity are indistinguishable."[20] This heroic "masculinity" needs to be acknowledged and accepted because this is the first step in transformation. The negative manifestation of this archetypal form is expressed in abusive power and domination. Priests need to move away from their insecurity and anxiety over these androgynous personality characteristics and begin to delve deeply into the spirituality of their own "femininity."

By accepting the feminine, by doing more than observing her plight from the height of our intellectual note-taking and head-shaking, and by recognizing that the physiological qualities we have deemed inferior are actually projections of our own psychological inferiority, we can restore our path to the androgyne. The physiological qualities which have been declared inferior and to belong to the feminine would now become psychological qualities appropriate to man or woman. Inferiority would no longer be only feminine, because we now see it as a part of a conjoined human consciousness; and the feminine would no longer be inferior, because it belongs to this structure of generally human consciousness.[21]

The Importance of Passivity

In *The Divine Milieu*, Pierre Teilhard de Chardin speaks eloquently concerning the importance of passivity as it relates to the spiritual life.

But can God also be found in and through every death? This is what perplexes us deeply. And yet this is what we must learn to acknowledge as a matter of settled habit and practice... unless we are prepared to forfeit commerce with God in one of the most widespread and at the same time most profoundly passive and receptive experiences of human life. The forces of diminishment are our real passivities.[22]

In Teilhard's mysticism, as in most others, receptivity, passivity, and descent (death) are primary experiences that enable a connection to God.

As I have noted, priesthood, even in its pre-Christian roots, has always been aligned with mediation. As spiritual theologian Louis Bouyer states, "priesthood ... is ... essentially mediation."[23] This mediatory function has a place as human beings relate to God, to nature, and to one another. It requires a priest, in the archetypal role of mediator, to be a living example of the reconciliation between masculine and feminine role stereotyping through an expression of androgyny.

This "middle function" is identified with an effeminate nature, and, says mythologist and psychologist Erich Neumann: "The interpretation of the priest or prophet as such an intermediate type is psychologically correct ..."[24] The historian of priesthood E.O. James maintains that priests needed to have some peculiarity prior to being qualified for this vocation.[25]

A Type of Border Crossing

As a part of this symbolic archetypal character, priests help people cross spiritual and psychic frontiers. This femininity in priesthood is a type of "border-crossing" phenomenon; an initiation into the mystical spirituality of which Teilhard speaks. Priests can choose to live in this marginal place between masculine and feminine roles. "The androgyne knows the difference between masculinity and femininity, and chooses to incorporate an owned portion of the opposite gender into his or her dominant identity."[26]

I suggest that Jesus is a paradigm of this androgyny. Contemporary spiritual theologians are discovering references to Jesus as feminine in the history of spirituality. Julian of Norwich writes, "In our Mother, Christ, we grow and develop ..."[27] The 12th-century Benedictine monk St. Anselm wrote: "And you, Jesus, are you not a mother?"[28] The supposition is that in the Christ we are neither male nor female. As Jung suggests,

Here the new androgynous form of existence becomes visible. Christianity is neither male nor female, it is male-female in the sense that the male paired with the female in Jesus' soul. In Jesus the tension and polaristic strife of sex are resolved in an androgynous unity. And the Church, as his heir, has taken this over from him: she too is androgynous.[29]

The priest, as mediator in this community called church, shares in the androgynous existence and becomes a model of it. This is related, too, to the sacrifice of Christ, whereby Jesus is crucified on a cross. Here is an identification with the primordial human.[30] This archetypal image unites the sacred and the profane, the male and the female, the darkness and the light. As Charles Poncé says, quoting Berdyaev, "The mystical life of the androgyne is realized not in one bisexual being but rather in the quadripartite union of two beings."[31] This represents the four-sidedness of the Cross.

This androgynous symbol is true of priests in many cultures.[32] For example, Siberian and North American shamans seem to have been able to integrate this into their lives and "border-crossing" priesthood.[33] A recent book called *The Zuni Man-Woman* by Will Roscoe, explains how this phenomenon was experienced in a Native American religion. A *berdache* was "a man who combined the work and social roles of men and women, an artist and a priest who dressed, at least in part, in women's clothes."[34]

These sanctified figures had multidimensional personalities and served in the traditional intermediate position of priesthood. They "were double sexed spirit guides... who moved freely in both the male and female social worlds and, as a result, helped both men and women reach greater understanding of each other and themselves."[35] The Jungian analyst, Robert Hopcke, has made this connection between the *berdache* and Catholic priests in his studies of the androgyne. He says that the enactment of the "not-man" identity by priests and monks "enables a greater contact with the mystical and ceremonial presence of the divine in human life."

> Undeniably, priests and monks ... find themselves involved in just those activities that were the domain of the *berdache* in Native American life: education, caretaking, and ceremonial and shamanistic duties.[36]

A Bridge Between Life and Death

Androgyny is seen in North American traditions as an initiatory bridge between life and death.[37] Biological sex did not dictate the roles that this person was to assume. In addition, one who undertook this religious career was to be passive and not supposed to engage in conflict. Two opposite qualities are combined in this figure of the androgyne, symbolizing humanity's original pre-gendered unity. These "feminine" priests are types of

> ... spirit guides capable of showing individuals and the community as a whole the way through this marginal terrain to new levels of social and psychological integration ... they become masters of two worlds, what (Victor) Turner calls "liminal personae" or "threshold" people. They appear at critical ritual and life-cycle junctures to usher the individual from one identity to another, from consciousness to unconsciousness and back.[38]

James Hillman describes this typology as a "soft man." It is related to the feminine symbolism that occurs at the passion of Jesus, where all humanity is exposed to a great strength in the weakness of God, which then becomes an example of compassion and understanding for all human weakness.[39] "In weakness power reaches perfection" (2

Corinthians 12:9). Priests need to accept this passivity as a nuclear component of their archetypal nature. In this way, perhaps the overriding need for patriarchal power would subside and the church could, indeed, become more universal.

This type of existence is militantly rejected in our contemporary culture. At the same time, many priests describe this type of personality structure in their lives. As an example, one priest told me of his awareness of this "feminine" component to his personality at a very early age. He liked doing stereotypical feminine things like ironing, washing the dishes and clothes, housekeeping, curling his grandmother's hair. He was also very sensitive and prone to passivity and deep emotion. The problem, of course, arises when church structures and society reject expression of this androgyne archetype. It then becomes relegated to the unconscious where it has the possibility of being altered into dominating power.

What Alfred Ziegler says concerning psychotherapy can also apply to priesthood:

> This passivity appears to belong to a special and particular form of service. It requires unusual training to avoid resorting to concrete action or activity of any sort but to withhold emotional energies to the point that they work invisibly behind the scenes.[39]

He goes on to say that this passivity seeks out the substance, the essential. Perhaps this is one reason why priesthood is being replaced by psychotherapy in our contemporary world, because priests have abandoned the passivity that leads to discovering the inner essence of Life.

> This humble attitude, an attitude which is aware of being an instrument in the hands of a power greater than itself, is the foundation-stone of ministry, the origins-attitude of the archetype of priest. If one begins a ministerial function with fantasies of ego-grandiosity he is out of harmony with his priestly pattern and is thus doomed to failure.[41]

A priest who accepts this needs to take on a receptive attitude, allowing the shapes and roles of this archetypal pattern to be transformed through his role as mediator. Here the passivity and androgynous nature of the priesthood can have positive archetypal effects. Each priest needs to open up the soul so that God's grace can be invoked. A priest needs to ask for help if the psychopathology is to be transformed. However, when the "power shadow" is dominant, priests can only focus on their ministry and their desire to give help to others. Ministerial activity is important, but cannot become central. Otherwise, power replaces love. Agape finds its substance in personal sacrifice and in passively letting go.

The Authentic Meaning of Celibacy

This primordial pattern of the androgyne also gives a clearer understanding of the legitimate meaning of celibacy, which symbolizes the archetype of purity that lies within the soul. Celibacy is not so much an external, physical practice as it is an inner, spiritual truth related to integrity.

> It means that we are healed through that part of ourselves which has remained uncontaminated by worldly considerations. That is the virgin in each of us, man and woman. It means that a secret part of ourselves (related to that "still, small voice of conscience") has remained pure, that is, true to its original disposition and unmoved by the allurements of the world which so effectively mold thought as well as behavior. The virgin, as our healing center, is more objective than our ego and adheres more consistently and resolutely to the truth. In that secret chamber of the soul new beginnings are continually being prepared.[42]

Perhaps priests will continue losing touch with this still, small voice of the heart as long as the church continues to insist on enforced celibacy merely as an external sexual discipline. Celibacy certainly is a very important need, primarily, though, because it reflects the integrity and clarity that lie deep within each person, that which makes one complete.

Celibacy is actually a charism that maintains the prototype of original human innocence.[43] This is the archetypal pattern that needs to be restored to the priesthood. Celibacy is a symbol of initiation.[44] As such, it needs to regain its authentic significance for all people, and not merely be literally applied just to priests. "Celibacy cannot survive as long as it is viewed simply as a restrictive law in the church or as something a priest is to live in isolation from his people."[45] Celibacy has become sexualized. In truth, it is an experience of the priestly archetype which expresses the mystical essence of integrity, the union of sexual opposites called androgyny. If priests could open themselves to experience this type of hidden genesis, sex would not be a problem. Priestly sexuality would no longer need to be repressed in the shadows of transgression.

Vanishing Differences

As we have seen, priests, when they are not compensating with abuses of power, are generally described in the research as feminine, passive, having aesthetic interests, unassertive, sensitive, creative, compliant, adaptable, altruistic, and receptive. Generally, priests seek abasement, nurturance, affiliation, and succorance.[46] All of this fits under the non-stereotyped term "role flexibility."[47] "Research has shown that androgynous individuals seem to have more flexible behavior patterns than people with more traditional masculine or feminine patterns."[48] Herein lies the primary importance of celibacy.[49] Priests can become examples to the world by expressing a flexibility of roles in all spheres: gender roles, sex roles, racial roles, cultural roles, ethnic roles, etc. This flexibility can become a sign that a person has received the indelible mark of priesthood.

And, it is precisely a refusal of this flexibility and adaptability that fragments into the "power shadow."[50] Role flexibility is central to the archetype of priestly androgyny. In order to respond positively to this pattern, priests need to give up the spirit of ego controlling, compensating patriarchy, and begin to honor the God of universal multiplicity.

It is on the cross that God experiences "the conflict peculiar to humanity, ... the conflict that is inherent in the disunity that expresses itself in suffering, and it is through this transformation that the androgyne appears in the person of Christ."[51] This androgynous archetypal pattern suggests that sacrifice and compassion are central to priesthood. This sacrifice is associated with the suffering that comes from experiencing separation and loss. It means that priests need to be docile and adaptable, and they need patient endurance, because, "we are weak and our need is great."[52]

Christ Is the Model

Fundamentally, priests are confronted with the necessity of mediating death, as we saw in our discussion of depression. This is essentially connected in Christianity to the Paschal Mystery, where Christ is a receptive figure who in the eyes of many was a failure and a fool. It has been called the scandal of the cross.

"The first thing that we have to do with heroism," says Ernest Becker in his book, *The Denial of Death*, "is to lay bare its underside ..." And "heroism is first and foremost a reflex of the terror of death."[53] Christ was certainly anti-heroic in his response to death. Denial of priestly androgyny is closely linked to this fear of sacrifice and death. Priests need to sacrifice ego needs with their associated heroic, "masculine," and patriarchal roots. By passively entering into their androgyny, priests can reconcile life and death.

Acceptance of androgyny also correlates with the cosmic nature of the priesthood. Priests are mediators of a universal life. As such, they need to become more resilient and withstand the temptation toward a one-sided way of existence. Accepting the preordained androgynous reality of this vocation can facilitate this process. Otherwise, priests only live out the negative "masculinized" dimension of this archetypal pattern, which is expressed as ego-heroic power, stemming from a compensatory and profound fear of sacrificial death.

Ironically, this fear is actually creating the death! As androgynous beings who embrace gender role flexibility, priests need to exemplify the sacrificial being in whom all are one: the Christ, in whom all differences vanish. "There does not exist among you Jew or Greek, slave or free, male or female. All are one in Christ Jesus" (Galatians 3:28).

CHAPTER SEVEN

From Passive Aggression to Living the Chaos

Part of the high cost of restoring the split archetype is having to contend with and finally sacrifice the kind of egocentricity that becomes horrendously inflated when one is trained for and lives out the priestly role in the church.[1]

These reflections have so far, touched on the conflicts and inconsistencies that are inherent in the priesthood. On the one hand, priests experience depression and apathy, while on the other hand they are perfectionistic and compulsive. The priesthood is described as having aggressive and antisocial qualities, while it also fits the profile of having androgynous and passive features. Priests show disordered symptoms that are dominant, compulsive, and powerful, while they also tend to be lethargic, submissive, and acquiescent. Of all the contradictions that are commonplace in priesthood, however, the most peculiar to priests is passive-aggressive temperament. And it usually emerges when a priest has not resolved the issue of role flexibility that is reflected in accepting the androgynous nature of this vocation.

A Well-Documented Issue

The disorder called passive-aggressive personality has been well documented in the priesthood. If anyone doubts that this pattern has archetypal significance, ask any priest who has lived with another in a rectory or community and you will hear story after story of passive-aggressive behavior. For example, angry priests can use silence to show their disfavor with someone. Or, they often utilize "prayer" and supposed forms of asceticism, which appear to be holy and upright, but are actually passive ways to keep others at a distance. Researchers, too, confirm the existence of passive-aggressive patterns in the priesthood.

Andrew Greeley, in his sociological study of priests in the United States, though he misses the important fact that priests are both aggressive and dependent, asserts:

> The indication is that one of the principal emotional deficiencies of priests is a slight tendency to be less able than others to cope with aggressive feelings; in other words, the priest is, if anything, more passive-aggressive than passive-dependent. If he has any tendency in passive directions it is to control others by his passivity. His neurotic style, when it exists, is more likely to be that of the "nice guy" rather than that of the dependent child.[2]

Seminarians consistently exhibit these symptoms in psychological testing.[3]

> [They] tend to be rather immature and narcissistic. They are emotionally passive, and they harbor very strong unrecognized dependency needs. They have difficulty incorporating societal values ... They are nonconforming ... A low frustration tolerance, coupled with intense feelings of anger and resentment, can lead to brief periods of aggressive acting out. Temporary remorse and guilt may follow the acting out behavior, but (these) persons are not likely to be able to inhibit similar episodes in the future.[4]

An Expression of Nonconformity

Another description of this disorder sees it as an expression of nonconformity where people want to defy social conventions in behavior and dress.[5] Many investigations confirm that seminarians and priests have passive-aggressive patterns in their behavior.[6] Ralph Dunn, after examining all of the MMPI research that had been done on seminarians over the years, concluded: "People reported on this review might have great capacity for passively accepting frustration ..."[7]

> There is evidence to indicate that the vocational decision of the "passive" person has been influenced by ego-oriented values unrelated to the vocational demands themselves... The passive person will tend to look for the kind of satisfactions which will give him ego-support, and he will tend to be domineering as a means of expressing the dominant qualities of leadership demanded by the vocation.[8]

This suggests that priests can become quite overbearing in their compensation for inner feelings of inadequacy, thus expressing the negative aspect of this passive-aggressive archetypal pattern. This is partly due to the excessive masculinization of our culture, where men are not expected to act passively.

The Center for Human Development describes 62% of the priests in its sample as denying anger and aggression, 57% experiencing anxiety concerning confrontation, and 68% viewing opposites as unrelated and antagonistic.[9] Priests are described as being high in reference to authority problems, are dogmatic and hostile, coupled with needs for dependency, passivity, deference, and nurturance, with low autonomy needs.[10] This includes passive-receptive and dependent qualities with autocratic authority conflicts.[11] Robert McAllister and Albert VanderVeldt refer to sexual acting out as related to these authority problems.[12] As suggested earlier, sexual acting out can become an unconscious way in which priests passively exhibit their anger and hostility toward authority figures who will be adversely affected by their sexual behavior.

> The value of being the proverbial gentle, meek, and mild person can become warped, allowing positive qualities to assume nega-

tive light. This tendency could explain why some priests, after a period of celibacy, compensate with an excessive exercise of power.[13]

Other studies verify the presence of strong passive-aggressive traits in the lives of priests.[14] Sean Sammon, in his study concerning stress and psychosocial development among clergymen, describes male religious professionals as having low ego identity coupled with authoritarianism.[15] In an examination of why priests leave the active ministry, it was concluded that the central issue is one of authority and powerlessness along with self-estrangement and isolation.[16] Passive-aggressive behavior is more likely to occur in systems where powerlessness is an issue.[17]

> While the minister is highest in the need to nurture, he also reveals his desire to bring people to accept his values ... While these studies indicate that there is an element of masculine desire to dominate among clergymen, other studies seem to come to opposite conclusions.[18]

In reality, the passivity and conformity found in priests might actually be a reaction against deep-seated feelings of hostility and rebellion. Herein lies a central contradiction in the archetype of priesthood.

Authority Problems and Power

Passive-aggressive personality is classically described as having a problem with authority. It "is characterized by passive resistance to demands for adequate social and occupational performance..."[19] "Passive-aggressive behaviors ... are highly common, especially where there is a hierarchy of authority and power."[20] In fact, passive-aggressive disorder was first studied as a phenomenon in the early 1950s in the U.S. military.

An essential feature of this personality style is passive resistance.[21] Basically, priests who are passive-aggressive do not trust authority figures, but outright expressions of anger, disapproval, or disagreement are shunned in favor of passive expressions of contradiction. And herein lies the chaos: priests basically do not trust their own inner authority and do not accept their own inner contradictions. All of the psychopathology that has been described in this book so far indicates this. The lack of self-acceptance leads to alienation from self, and it becomes externally expressed in estrangement from the realities of life. Primarily, it is an alienation from the very archetype of priesthood. This is a fundamental issue that needs to be reconciled in the lives of priests.

Paradoxically, priests want to belong to hierarchies and to be in positions of authority, but they also do not trust authority.[22] Actually, priests do not accept and trust the paradoxical nature of their own uncertain beings: that they are depressed and perfectionistic, passive and aggressive. This lack of inner confidence can lead to hierarchical fascism.

Passive-aggressive patterns both establish themselves and ripen in hierarchical systems. "Organized religion typically is an 'ideal' environment for the development and nurturance of passive-aggressiveness."[23] Louis Breger writes that hierarchies grow out of a need to curb aggression.

> Some means was required which would allow aggressive individuals to live together in close groups without tearing each other apart—some means of controlling and redirecting aggression. Dominance hierarchies were evolution's solution to this problem.[24]

Hierarchies are exemplified by "prejudice toward outsiders, on the one hand, and intolerance and ostracism of group members who deviate from conventionally defined ways of life, on the other."[25] This is very likely the reason why priests engage in these disordered and negative archetypal patterns: whenever a priest tries to advance any creativity, offers a differing opinion, or disagrees with the hierarchically determined dogmatic theology or power, that priest is emotionally, and sometimes physically, banished. So, priests, in their fear, tend to develop passive ways to express their disagreement and their creativity. A cursory view of history supports this supposition. Many of the saints in the history of the Roman Catholic Church are examples of this exile. Only years after these "rebels" have died are they considered "saints."[26] Many, when they are alive, threatened the power of the hierarchical system.

A False Type of Harmony

From an institutional point of view, this passive-aggressive behavior can produce a false type of harmony. Moreover, it has a very high price: "ethnocentrism and intolerance of human differences."[27] Therefore, this type of institutionalized hierarchy is actually anti-catholic, not allowing for the universal differences that exist in creation. Hierarchical control through conformity can create an environment where priests will tend to dissociate themselves from feelings of assertion and disagreement, causing a split to take place in their psychological and spiritual makeup.

Being passive in one's aggression means that one does not have to be ostracized. It also means, though, that a priest will continue in the negative archetypal pathology of this disorder: immaturity, narcissism, repressed anger, resentfulness, bitterness, sexual acting-out, indecisiveness, and irresponsibility. In the final analysis, these passive-aggressive priests join in the hierarchical power and become authoritarian themselves, in many ways becoming what they hate. Thus, their priestly leadership and mediation are ineffective.

In order for a positive archetypal resolution to occur, priests need to develop an awareness that aggression is instinctual and quite appropriate to their vocation. This is verified by the famous ethologist and student of human behavior, Conrad Lorenz.

> The point of Lorenz's book, *Das Sogenannte Bose* (literally "so-called evil," translated with the rather misleading English title *On Aggression*), is to deny that aggression is evil or unnatural. Aggression, the general tendency to attack, is, he suggests, by no means a tendency to destroy—which in fact in normal conditions it seldom does.[28]

This, it seems, is usually the reason why hierarchical structures have anxiety about aggression: they fear destruction. So, because the hierarchical system dreads losing its power, it exerts even more control over its members. And, because individual priests fear rejection and ostracism, they refrain from advancing their own imaginative ideas and disagreements. This prevailing disorder needs to be addressed and accepted if the priesthood is ever to regain its archetypal significance.

When ethnocentrism (belief in the superiority of one's own group), prejudice, preservation of an "in-group," secrecy, and fear of destruction are at their zenith, we can certainly expect, in compensation, a greater display of abusive power from those who are not "in."[29] This pattern of passive-aggressive "harmony" is not ultimately of service in terms of maintaining a healthy institution. It is based on fear, which is the hallmark of deficient faith.[30] In truth, what priests and the hierarchical organizations fear most is their own inner weakness, which could actually serve their assertive creativity if they would allow it to be transformed. It is through this very weakness that God's ingenious grace can act. This fear, however, because it is not openly confronted, is facilitating the ultimate destruction of the priesthood.

Whenever an institution such as the hierarchical priesthood thinks itself to be idealistically and one-sidedly peaceloving and passive, there may appear to be no other response pattern except passive-aggression. In fact, this style of relating begins to seem necessary for survival. Hierarchical authority will demand it. Breger describes this situation in relationship to our U.S. society in general:

> Somehow, over the course of our history, Americans have acquired the belief that we are a peaceful, innocent people who fight only when provoked or attacked. Nothing could be further from the truth. We believe in our innocence in spite of the fact that we are among the most intensely competitive, driving, success-oriented people that ever lived.[31]

In the priesthood, this coincides with the perfectionistic, obsessive-compulsive style that was discussed earlier. Priests are very competitive, especially in relationship to one another. This competition, as with other dominating and potent actions, is hidden under an umbrella of acquiescence and nonresistance. If it existed openly and honestly it would not be destructive, because it could forge dialogue, relationship, and personal exchange (remember that "aggress" means "to advance toward," "to draw closer to"). Real cooperation could come about, whereby priests would honor their own creativity, differences, diversity, and mediate the same in others.

Having and Being

Erich Fromm, in his book, *To Have Or To Be*, describes a type of dichotomy that could be helpful to the transformation of priesthood. For Fromm, "having" is passivity ("passivating" is his word), which, he says, comes from a need for power. It is centered on things; it finds its expression in incorporation, consumption, possession, and submission. "Having" is associated with hierarchical structures of survival, dominance, authoritarianism, and heroic exploits.

> Having consists of formulations created by others... One submits to others, usually a bureaucracy ... The having mode of existence ... produces the desire—indeed, the need—for power.[32]

This paradoxical formulation of having and passivity fits the concepts of archetypal priesthood. Priests can become adept at painting a sweet veneer over feelings and behaviors like control, power, anger, dominance, and conflict. Robert Wicks proposes some classic ways in which priests do this: sometimes through their preaching, throwing hints, writing memos, justification, pseudo-forgiveness (so the other can't respond by being angry), resentment, and hidden agendas.[33] Go to any religious house or rectory where several priests are living together and you will invariably find this "memo writing syndrome." The other symptoms can be discovered wherever a priest has made a mistake or feels out of control. Ideas such as martyrdom, sacrifice, discipline, and salvation can get used in order to promote passive-aggressive attitudes of "having."

In this distortion, a tendency in the direction of "having" can cause a priest to become compromised, consumed, and possessed by the hierarchical framework. Priestly integrity is jeopardized. In this sense, then, Fromm might say that a priest can frankly believe that he is free, when in fact he is being manipulated.[34] This conditioning is related to anxiety concerning ostracism: "... human beings are more afraid of being outcasts than even of dying."[35]

In contrast to the "having" mode of existence, Fromm postulates "being." "Being" is life, activity, birth, renewal, outpouring, flowing out, productivity. It is related to aggression in that it is an advance toward. "Being is the opposite of having, of ego-boundness and egotism."[36] "Being" is process, movement, experience, ambivalence, nonauthoritarian and imaginative. "To be requires ... making oneself empty and poor, giving up."[37] It is interesting to note here how Fromm shifts meanings: "having" is non-dynamic whereas "being" is animated. In order to aggress, one must let go of whatever has been hanging on. "Being" is a form of integrity.

The Need For Emptiness and Chaos

The priesthood needs this emptiness and chaos. Meister Eckhart, a Dominican mystic of the Middle Ages, called it "action through non-action," a form of letting go of oneself.[38] It requires a falling into grace. This type of activity lets grace happen but at the same time is not passive. A priest who accepts this type of ambivalence is one who takes action, who aggresses. This state of "being," however, does not need to use the "power shadow": domination, authoritarianism, or hierarchical control. There is no force, and yet there is vigor, potency, strength, assertion, and energy. A priest needs to live this creative chaos.

"In the beginning ... the earth was a formless wasteland, and darkness covered the abyss, while a mighty wind swept over the waters" (Genesis 1:1–2). This phrase captures images having to do with the transformation that is needed in the priesthood today. This mighty wind is the dynamic first cause of creation. It advances life. Priests need to get in touch with the formless, dark, depressed, perfectionistic, passive, antisocial wasteland of their own souls. It is precisely here that the positive archetypal energy imprints the priesthood with its indelible mark. For Christianity, this is reflected in the contradiction of the cross.

> Christ's crucifixion is replete with images of splitting and coming apart. The Veil of the Temple rent in twain, the piercing of his side, the darkness at noon, the blood and water running out as separate elements. He showed that we must risk coming apart to be reintegrated, lose our life to save it ... As we let these conflicts tear us, we become painfully aware of the values involved and of our responsibility for the quality and disproportion of those contending forces.[39]

The priesthood today desperately needs to get in touch with this splitting, with this chaotic emptiness, with this "coming apart" so that it can experience the transformation which awaits. Fear will not prevent this from happening because, in God's "foolish" design, the dynamic is already at work and has been for some time. The priesthood as we know it is dying. Its contradictions are becoming more and more apparent to the world. But if we follow the way of creation and the cross, we believe that this upheaval is merely the metamorphosis toward new life. Priests need to embrace the contradictions and grow within them.

An expert on passive-aggressive patterns has said that "this style is seen as passive in aggression but active in ambivalence."[40] This idea leads us into the true archetypal roots of priesthood, which is the subject of the next chapter.

CHAPTER EIGHT

From Contradiction
to Ambivalence

"To become acquainted with oneself is a terrible shock."[1]

As we have seen, the pall surrounding priesthood today has been described in many ways. The U.S. Catholic Bishops have called it low morale. I suggest that this low point is very significant in the history of priesthood because it is a call to see the deeper, archetypal roots of this vocation. Throughout this book, I have suggested that contradictions have been discussed as trials and transformations. These include:

from depression to contemplative emptiness; from worry to grace; from authoritarian control to upholding tradition; from isolation to mysticism; from apathy to forgiveness; from lethargy to forgetfulness; from insecurity to faith; from aloofness to alteration; from distance to intimacy; from unsociability to freedom;

from pessimism to woundedness; from sadness to penance; from grief to the good shepherd; from withdrawal to reflection; from self-deprecation to meditation; from perfection to imperfection; from all-or-nothing to reconciliation; both/and; from dogmatism to mercy; from workaholism to affection; from moralism to invalidism; from compulsion to compassion; from narcissistic indifference to passionate involvement; from power to love; from arrogance to absolution; from isolation to familiarity; from stereotypes to flexibility; from indecisiveness to responsibility; from passivating to aggression; from dogmatism to powerlessness; from order to chaos.

These contradictions offer a glimpse of the true archetype of priesthood, because each actually has a place in the indelible mark of this vocation.

Jung maintained that ambivalence is the most characteristic feature of an archetype.[2] This is also true for the archetype of priesthood. Denying the darker aspects, however, as is presently happening in the church, is only serving to exaggerate the "power shadow." If this keeps up it will cause the very dissolution of priesthood. Because this vocation is primarily one of mediation; priests have the grave responsibility of allowing the contradictions within their own lives to be mediated. This does not seem to be happening at the present time.

As stated earlier, *The Center For Human Development* reports that "68% of priests view opposites as unrelated and antagonistic."[3] If priests do not begin to accept their own inner, archetypal ambivalence, the pathological disorders I have been describing will destroy their sense of call. An ambivalent personality is contradictory and erratic, alternating between dependence and independence. This experience of malleability is the one dynamic that penetrates to the very core of priesthood, and it has the potential to destroy it or to enliven it. The priesthood is a paradox.

All of the disorders we have discussed involve ambivalence, as is obvious from the list above. This conflicting archetypal pattern is both seductive and repulsive. It is depressed and perfectionistic, apathetic and domineering. It changes forms from martyr to savior, from misunderstood to contrite, from advocate to aggrieved.[4]

Two Sides of Ambivalence

One type of ambivalence is deadly, while another is creative. To borrow Fromm's categories, we can discover an "ambivalence of having" and an "ambivalence of being." In the first category, ambivalence creates fear and a compensatory need for power. This is an overriding desire to control through fear and indifference. "Ambivalence of having" is a real temptation for a priest. A priest who practices it uses indecision and uncertainty as passive methods of domination in order to make others submit, or to possess others, or to have them remain incorporated and conditioned by a hierarchical framework.

This type of priesthood is *laissez-faire*. It fears conflict and is irresolute. It does not lead to mediation. It rules through the principle of "divide and conquer." The basic need exemplified by an "ambivalence of having" is the need for security. It is based on fear and is not priestly. If it is maintained, it will only continue to focus the priesthood on the trials that afflict it.

The other type of ambivalence can be called an "ambivalence of being." Here, the primary need is to be filled. It is an empty ambivalence. The priest who lives in this state is a receptive instrument of grace. This ambivalence is creative; it allows for chaos, void, assertion, and conflict as precursors to creation. It is engaging, relational, and develops imagination; by falling into grace it aggresses. This empty passivity allows God to act; it mediates God.

Indeed "the ambivalence of being" is *the* attitude of a mediator! The negative archetypal dynamic can take over when priests do not acknowledge and accept this reality. Priesthood today is, in fact, being given a very strong message concerning its archetypal roots. It is being plunged into the depths of its own emptiness. Hence, the overriding emphasis on psychological treatment for disorders, the low morale, the shortages of vocations, the uncertainty, and the mixed emotions. Panic around these symptoms can lead to an overwhelming anxiety, which will try to stop this immersion through any means. In the end, though, this fear will not triumph.

Mediatory "ambivalence of being" is the gift that priesthood needs to contribute to the world.

It is one of Lorenz's most interesting suggestions that only creatures capable of aggression toward their own kind are capable of affection. Ambivalence may be ancient indeed![5]

This "ambivalence of being" lies deep within the nature and function of priesthood. It is the foundation of faith, of knowing by unknowing, of action through nonaction. Herein lies the meaning of the message: love your enemies.

It has many practical consequences. For example, in this age of committees and meetings, many priests are frustrated by their apparent lack of authority. To act as a priest who employs this archetypal concept of ambivalence, however, one would need to enter every meeting or planning session "empty." In this way, mediation would become truly possible, because the priest would be letting go of personal agendas. With this demeanor it is guaranteed that the meeting would have creative results. These conclusions may not suit everyone, but reconciliation is the essential core of living together in peace.

Discovering the Grace

Priests who can embrace this receptive, mediatory stance will gather up the fragments of these disorders and discover the grace that is present in the pieces, particularly in the archetypal fragments that are contradictory. They will then be able to help others pick up the pieces of *their* fragmented lives, and empower them to accept the wonderful mystery and diversity of humanity.

Profound truth is always contradictory, just as a great love is always ambivalent. Passion makes us capable of giving our lives for the other, but also of taking the life of the beloved. There are no two ways about it: where there is no conflict, neither is there love.[6]

All of the conflict surrounding priesthood today is a real gift from God. Perhaps it is within this context, too, that inner celibacy really takes on its meaning. "Ambivalence goes deep; it must be respected and understood."[7] Ambivalence is Life! Priests need to regain their position as mediators of this truth. Priesthood is a vocation of openness, and this attitude needs to flow through and pervade all aspects of a priest's life. Priesthood, if it is indelible, must, paradoxically, embrace its chaos. It is a vocation that can reveal the dark and shadowy side of personal pathology, so that these shadows can be transformed. This darkness is a call, an initiation rite, for each individual priest.

> Despite the current emphasis on "the ministry of the laity," nothing changes in the church until the priest changes ... The wound to be addressed is deep within the psyche of the priest where ... the archetypes have been split and a terrible price has been paid for the unconscious one-sidedness. It is incumbent upon the priest to reclaim the shadow side that longs for absolution ... The illness born of that feeling of being special is reinforced by seminary, parish, and even family until, from deep within, God's wrath erupts ... Only when a priest experiences transformation can a call by God be discerned in a new way as a call to a deeper ministry.[8]

Mystical death is required; a confrontation with the disordered shadows that lie within this vocation. A great religious crisis is being placed at the feet of each priest, a personal "agony in the garden." Reflective musing can take one into the deeper recesses of the soul where these archetypal fragments of being can be accepted. This is the first step in the initiation. "We all know ... that unless we attend to our inner conflicts and contradictions, not only will we find ourselves torn apart by our inner divisions but also we shall very likely inflict wounds on those around us."[9]

The priesthood today does not need some type of idealistic, escapist healing or a return to habitual trappings. Priests need to contemplate the inner contradictions. By holding this chaos, the grace of God's aggressive and creative hand will refashion the indelible mark. "What was by nature empty and void, a return to bits and pieces, can, in any human existence, become fullness and unity in God."[10] Living with contradictions and ambivalence offers the possibility of discovering the deep archetypal nature of this vocation.

> The function of death is to provide the necessary entrance into our inmost selves. It will make us undergo the required dissocia-

tion. It will put us into the state organically needed if the divine fire is to descend upon us.[11]

This is a function of the heart. "As we learn to live with paradox we have to admit that two realities may be equally true ... The mind will never apprehend the truth of paradox. Only the heart can do that."[12]

The Illusion of Wholeness

We have come to accept the notion of wholeness as meaning the absence of contradictions in a self or a system. Our society is replete with wholistic ideas about spirituality, therapy, and life. These beliefs are an illusion. This search for completeness is similar to the hopes expressed in the time of Jesus by people who were seeking a political messiah. Messianism is intended to bring about universal peace. For many of us, this peace has been interpreted politically, and now spiritually, as the absence of division or variation. This political wholeness is a fallacy. It is a form of pride that wants everyone and everything to be the same. It is death. Yet, it is strongly emphasized in our society by hierarchical psychology and social theories, which have relegated to themselves much of the power that is being taken away from the priesthood. The concept of "wholeness" needs to be understood as an acceptance of diversity, both within a person and within a community, rather than as some idealized unity. The only true integrity comes from accepting personal ambivalence and paradox.

The messianic Christ did aggressively encounter and confront division and darkness. This messiah was opposed to the hatred that caused splitting and division and is evident in the animosity shown to the priests of the time, the Scribes and Pharisees. When priests hate the opposing forces in their own life, love for their enemies is impossible.

This is essentially why the Scribes and Pharisees were so judgmental and moralistic toward others. They were unable to accept their own inner darkness and allow it to mediate the message of truth. Therefore, they were not messianic, priestly, or prophetic leaders. In their fear, they projected onto others all of their own pathologies. As do the priests of today, they separated themselves from the balance of humanity. It is this type of separation that the Christ opposed and condemned.

Priests cause true hatred when they resist the diversity and ambivalence of life by imposing their power with authoritarian expectations. As we have seen, this usually stems from inner inferiority and an inability to accept the contradictions in their own lives. This kind of hatred is diametrically opposed to the messianic and universal meaning of peace and wholeness (integrity). Only when a priest is able to gracefully accept personal disparity deep within his own soul can he accept the same diversity and ambivalence in others. Love of enemies will be possible.

The Role of God's Grace

As this becomes a reality, however, the real division of which Christ speaks is bound to happen within the structures of society and the church (cf. Matthew 10:34). This division, which is essential to the messianic message, is caused by the acceptance of diversity, fluidity, and role flexibility, all of which are mediated through the grace of God's paradoxical nature. It is a division in which some priests will be ostracized by the institution; in which priests may be at odds with one another because their hierarchical power is threatened.

Those priests, however, who seek only security and who want everyone and everything to be the same, to be whole, pure and perfect, will continue to languish in their own negative trials and symptoms, because they fear the intimacy that this unity in diversity implies. True wholeness can come about only when contradiction and ambivalence are embraced (cf. 1 Corinthians 12:4–11). If a priest wishes to protect his power, and if he fears being shut out, this dynamic, aggressive transformation cannot happen.

The mystery of the eucharist, which is the summit of the Christian life, the sacred action surpassing all others, has meaning in this context.

> Then taking a cup he offered a blessing in thanks and said: "Take this and *divide* it among you ..." Then, taking bread and giving thanks, he *broke it* and gave it to them saying: "This is my body given for you, do this in remembrance of me" (Luke 22:17–19).

The dividing and the breaking are pivotal actions for everyone who wants to understand the true meaning of Eucharist.

So, too, this symbol of brokenness is essential in understanding the priesthood. Whenever the archetype of this broken and divided God is mediated, priests are fulfilling the indelible mark of their vocation. As we have seen, however, priests tend to deny and repress this brokenness within themselves and the fractured community. They often prefer an illusion of undefinable oneness. They set themselves up for the negative manifestations of the priestly archetype in self-righteousness and pomposity.

Life is a mystery of ambivalence. True humility is an ability to live with ambiguity. Priesthood is a vocation that is graced with a permanent "thorn in the flesh," and its role is to live out and preach this traditional truth. In this way, real security is manifested as faith, a gift which accepts and lives with all of the changes, all of the surprises, and all of the contradictions of life. Only the Christ can give meaning to the incongruity of life. He is Emmanuel, God with us. He is the one that priests, if they have the indelible and paradoxical mark, are invited to mediate. This can happen only when priests begin to freely empty themselves of their fears and false security, allowing Christ to mediate life through their personal contradictions and ambivalence.

CHAPTER NINE

An Initiation Rite

Man's anxiety is a function of his sheer ambiguity and of his complete powerlessness to overcome that ambiguity, to be straightforwardly an animal or an angel.[1]

Angels and Hearts

Belief in angels has definitely waned within institutionalized religions over the past thirty years. This image, however, seems to be resurfacing in other areas such as "new age" theories. Angels have always been recognized as creatures who deliver a message of ambivalence: they go up and down at the same time, they are in and out, they are observer and observed. They are androgynous,[2] examples of self-emptying and of immortality. In these marvelous creatures "... one set of values contains the other within it."[3] In a very real sense all of the negative symptoms we have described in this book are true angelic messengers.

Priests lack a vision of angels who can liberate (Genesis 48:16) and who can lead (Exodus 23:20), who can deliver the message of truth

(Judges 6:11–22); guardian angels who will act as intermediaries for them with God in their vocation of mediation. The pathologies of priesthood *are* these intermediaries. As suggested, priests need to let go of their ego-controlling ways and become emptied. Angels can deliver priests from the fear of living out this holy "ambivalence of being." Angels can appear to each priest offering courage in this time of chaos and upheaval. Angels can convey the message that this is not the priest's work or the priest's mediation, but is aggressive grace being reconciled through empty souls.

One of my favorite hymns as a child was "Panis Angelicus." Here translated from the Latin, the words are astonishing.

> The bread of angels has become the
>   bread of people;
> The heavenly bread brings an end to
>   the symbol:
> What a marvelous event!
> The poor, the slaves, the humble eat their Lord.
> We beg you, one triune Godhead,
> Hence you visit us as we worship you;
> By your ways lead us,
>   who are tending
> Toward the light that you inhabit.
> Amen.[4]

The bread of angels has become the bread of people. Such ambivalence: the poor and the humble eat their God. This is the function and the archetype of priesthood, to mediate this mysterious truth!

The Image of the Sacred Heart

Another image that is central to understanding the transformation of priesthood is the Sacred Heart. Each priest needs to unearth his own blessedness of heart. The psalms, which priests pray with and for the community each day, are replete with this ambivalent symbol: the thoughts of the heart, the mischief of the heart, the innocence of the heart, the upright heart, the truth of the heart, a loyal heart, the joy of the heart, the sorrow of the heart, and so on. Hearts are, indeed, the seat of contradiction and ambivalence, the core of life. Priesthood needs to mediate the wisdom that every heart is sacred as it holds all of this paradox.

> One day, while I was before the Blessed Sacrament, and having at the time more leisure than usual, I felt myself wholly invested in the presence of God. Thus I lost all thought of myself and the place where I was ... surrendering my heart to the power of his love. My Sovereign Master granted me to repose for a long time upon his divine breast, where he uncovered to me the marvels of his love, and the inexplicable secrets of his Sacred Heart, which he had hitherto concealed from me. He opened for me for the first time his divine heart.[5]

This account of the vision of Margaret Mary Alacoque in 1673 is a preamble to the needs of the modern world. In a second vision, Margaret Mary sees the cross implanted in the Sacred Heart. We today are familiar with the image of the Sacred Heart wrapped in a crown of thorns. "It would seem that when our hearts 'stutter' we stumble and fall."[6] The ambivalence of the heart could lead priests to the gold, if only they could surrender their own ego core.

The heart is connected to many systems in the human body. Without it there is no life. It is also a symbol of relatedness. As we have seen in discussing all of the disorders of priesthood, priests are in desperate need of human intimacy.

> The heart is not complete without an arterial system. But an arterial system, with its branches of veins, arteries, and capillaries, is precisely what our contemporary society rejects because it implies connections, links, ties and obligations ... Our society is not heartless as much as it is "cordless."[7]

This gives a fairly good insight into the needs of the priesthood in the contemporary world. The Latin, *cord*, is part of words like cordial, concord, discord, record, and courage. The symbol of the heart takes us to the core of our being, our integrity. It also echoes the word belief, *credere*.[8] It implies an endorsement of personal brokenness by each and every priest. "All forms of being 'beside oneself,' of chaos, belong to the rhythm and harmony of the heart."[9] As William James, in his classic work, *The Varieties of Religious Experience,* states in relation to the heart: "A little irritable weakness and descent of the pain-threshold will bring the worm at the *core* of all our usual springs of delight into full view..."[10] The worm of brokenness, of a broken heart, can be the prime mediator leading priests to connect to their own painful, inner contradictions and, following this, to the ambivalence of life in general. Only a heart can understand paradox.

Symbolic of the Cross

The Sacred Heart is symbolic of the cross. Priests need to accept the contradictions of life as a crucifixion if the core of this vocation is to be transformed. This means that priests must begin to accept differences within themselves and then within the community. The cross is not so much a symbol of suffering as it is a standard of the passion which comes from transcending dichotomies. "An intolerance of differences results in a divided heart."[11] Divided hearts have no passion. Acceptance of contradictions and ambivalence can form the passion, the ardor, and the affection that priests need.

In the 14th century, Meister Eckhart, one of the greatest preachers of the mystery of the Heart of Jesus, wrote these words: "On the cross his Heart burnt like a figure and a furnace from which the flame burst forth on all sides. So was he inflamed on the cross by his fire of love for the whole world.[12]

Priests need to pray for their own hearts to be engulfed in these flames so that they can burst forth in proclaiming the great mystery and folly of paradoxical truth. This is the contradiction of the cross. "The message of the cross is complete absurdity to those who are headed for ruin..." but to those who believe, "the power of God and the wisdom of God. For God's folly is wiser than people, and God's weakness more powerful than people" (1 Corinthians 1:18–25).

Such a redefinition of priesthood in both priest and lay person does not happen by changing titles or learning more about moving the sanctuary furniture or building a new cathedral. It happens inside. When it does, people have the vision and power to change the world, for the goal is not to renew or save the church —the agenda is the human soul and even life on this planet.[13]

A New Arrangement

The archetype of priesthood molds dichotomous realities into a new arrangement. This is a function of transcendence. Abraham Maslow says,

> Dichotomizing pathologizes and pathology dichotomizes... Isolating two interrelated parts of a whole from each other, parts that need each other, parts that are truly "parts" and not wholes, distorts them both, sickens and contaminates them.[14]

Dichotomized religion is doomed, says Maslow, because it "tends to become arbitrary and authoritarian ... The sacred needs to infuse all of life and not be compartmentalized." Dichotomizing, he concludes, has pathologized organized religion.[15] As we have seen, the priesthood has a primary purpose of handing on or mediating opposing forces of life. This requires transcendence, a recognition that some mystery beyond human understanding does the actual mediation. It is the role of priesthood to ritualize this mystery and to create the transitional space where people can celebrate their diversity. Priesthood is a vocation that is intended to transcend dichotomies.

Marsha Sinetar, writing about how ordinary people can become mystics, says, "Both social and self transcendence involve a letting go of the old secure ways."[16] Jung calls this synthesizing of ambivalent forces the "transcendent function." Conveying the message of transcendence is central to priesthood.

Rejoice in the Dying
　　But this:
　　to contain death
　　even before life has begun
　　to contain it so gently
　　and not to be angry—
　　this is indescribable.[17]

Priesthood needs to rejoice at its own demise. This is the most basic and almost impossible contradiction to accept. Every contemporary priest needs to let go of priesthood in order to rediscover it! Priesthood must die in order to experience transformation. Priests mediate; they help people cross mystical borders, back and forth, from death to life to death ... If priesthood cannot accept its own paradoxical death then it will never fully come to life in this age. *Border-crossing mediation* is the archetype of priesthood.

In defining an archetype, David Miller says that it combines remembering, contemplation, and loving. It does the work, he says, of "leading back."[18] This is the way for priesthood to enter into this transmutation, going back into the recesses of its primordial foundations.

The Need To Reconnect

"Re-membering means nothing if not re-connecting," says Catherine Keller.[19] Priesthood needs to reconnect with its roots if is to encounter new life. Contemplation can make this happen. Priests need to ponder their depression, their perfectionism, their "power shadows," their passivity, their aggression, and their androgynous role. They are being called to accept their humanity; to view with passion all that is within them and around them. This is the meaning of *contemplare*, to be in place where one can observe the meaning of things. They are called to do this, but see meaning in the ambiguity within and around them. Priests are being challenged to look around and to see within and beyond their psychopathology to the grace of revitalization.

Contemplation leads down into the depths of the heart where the true meaning of this ambiguity and diversity can be discovered. It will lead each priest to identify personal disorders, discovering precisely where the initiation begins, in the grace of acceptance.

And in the light of this grace we perceive the power of grace in our relation to ourselves. We experience moments in which we accept ourselves, because we feel that we have been accepted by that which is greater than we. If only more such moments were given to us! For it is such moments that make us love our life, that make us accept ourselves, not in our goodness and self- complacency, but in the certainty of the eternal meaning of our life. We cannot force ourselves to accept ourselves. We cannot compel anyone to accept himself (sic). But sometimes it happens that we receive the power to say "yes" to ourselves, that peace enters into us and makes us whole, that self-hate and self-contempt disappear, and that ourself is reunited with itself. Then we can say that grace has come upon us.[20]

The Service of Transformation

Sacrifice means "to perform the sacred." This performance is going on today in the lives of priests who are disordered, and it is, indeed, sacred. These priests, who are considered to be problems by the hierarchy, or who are rejected and shunned because of their disorders and diseases, can give a fundamental example to the self-righteous among us. They have accepted the shadow side of themselves and can be transformed. In the French usage of sacred we find its contradictory, double meaning. *Sacré* implies the connotation of being cursed. When a priest begins to encounter the afflictions and disordered symptoms of this vocation, an initiation has begun.

But, there is a grave danger here. Prudence, calmness, and discretion are needed so that fear does not control the process. It is a period of deep discernment and not a time for romanticism or sentimentalism. As Robert Bly suggests, the Shadow needs to be absorbed and eaten.[21] This is the sacrificial communion. The "power shadow" of sociopathy is lurking in the transformation. Antisocial feelings can be very strong. A new arrogance can emerge that regards the wounded priest as a savior. There can be a temptation to see this transformation process merely as magic, gifting the priest with supernatural energy. Priests need to be aware of this trap so that they are not overcome by the temptation. This, too, is very much a part of their mediatory vocation: being always able to see the other side of any experience. *Everything* has a shadow side (including the ideas in this book).

Sacrifice is a very dangerous move without awareness of shadow. So, the performance of this initiation contains both blessing and curse, the beginnings of the contradictory nature of this vocation. It is here that Jung's transcendent function can come into play. The ambivalent and paradoxical symbols of love and death, eros and thanatos, need to be experienced as one reality.

Psychopathic deviance, as Guggenbuhl-Craig suggests, is "eros on crutches." It does not connect. Therefore, it needs the sacrificial transformation. Then a priest can develop compassion.

The image of the Christ as mediator, as sacrificer and sacrificed all contained within one personal encounter, is a sound metaphor: the humiliation, death, burial, descent into hell, resurrection, ascension, and gift of the Holy Spirit are one multiple reality, experienced in a dynamic field of many interacting forces; always happening and re-happening. Care needs to be taken not to become fixated on either the humiliation or the resurrection. As mentioned earlier, the priest, too, is sacrifice and sacrificer. Here, then, is the transcendence that turns pathology into an authentic vocation.

Welcoming Darkness

A true priest is able to welcome and embrace the disordered darkness in a consuming communion, in which the word "consume" is understood as meaning "to take upon oneself by choice."[22] This expansion of personality means that a priest is no longer stuck in the pathological shadows of this archetypal vocation but is able to flow with the ambivalent contradictions that contain and hold the indelible mark of priesthood.

He must celebrate a Last Supper with himself, and eat his own flesh and drink his own blood; which means that he must recognize and accept the other in himself. But if he persists in his one-sidedness, the two lions will tear each other to pieces. Is this perhaps the meaning of Christ's teaching, that each must bear his own cross? For if you have to endure yourself, how will you be able to rend others also?[23]

Another way of putting this comes from Jesus: "I solemnly assure you, unless a grain of wheat falls to the earth and dies, it remains just a grain of wheat. But if it dies it produces much fruit" (John 12:24).

So, this death is the work of life and this life the work of death, because transformation cannot take place without the procedure of nature. It is an experience that is common to the entire created universe and yet a mystery nonetheless.

I said to my soul, be still, and wait without hope
For hope would be hope for the wrong thing; wait
    without love
For love would be love for the wrong thing; there is
    yet faith
But the faith and love and the hope are all in the
    waiting.
Wait without thought, for you are not ready for
    thought:
So the darkness shall be the light, and the stillness
    the dancing.[24]

In this process the priesthood will become blessed. The word, "to bless," also has some contradictory and ambivalent meanings. It comes from an Old English derivation of bloody, to consecrate with blood.

In French, *blesser* is "to wound," and as Jacob said to the angel who wounded him in the joint of his race progenitor's thigh, "I will not let you go unless you bless me" (Genesis 32:26). Is the angel, who must be held on to like Proteus, the divinity of the soul image, who both wounds and blesses? Is wounding equivalent in some way to "being blessed"?[25]

Mediating God's Love

Yes, indeed! And so, being blessed by all of this pathology, a priest can mediate God's contradictory, paradoxical, and wounded love to others.

The total "soul" of a person embraces everything within the circle of life, everything around that person. If the soul is strong, it must leave an impression on all its undertakings ... Blessing is the soul's power that produces all progress *(salah)*. This means it is related to wisdom ... The act of blessing, *berekh*, means imparting vital power to another person. The one who blesses gives the other person something of his own soul.[26]

Enduring the sacrificial passions that are aroused through connection, contemplation, and love means that the priesthood can traverse the contradiction of death/life and mediate this border crossing for others. The priesthood then embraces its archetypal nature as a wonderful, transforming death/life in itself: insecure, temperamental, capricious, passive, aggressive, latent, inverted, animated, vulnerable, conditional, tentative, malleable, developing, and sustaining.

As Miller points out, this process is a "dark night," a "night that is illumination," a "superluminous darkness." He then goes on to quote Meister Eckhart:

> The light shines in the darkness and there a person becomes aware of it... It is when people are in the dark, or suffering, that they are to see the light. Truth is that the more we see ourselves as we are, the less (ego-) self is in us.[27]

Let us pray that the priests of our time will enter into the darkness of their own disordered pathology, suffer and die to ego, so that their indelible mark can be rediscovered and they can be transformed.

Notes

Introduction

1. Fox, Thomas C. (1995). *Sexuality and Catholicism*. New York: George Braziller, p. 166.

CHAPTER ONE—FROM ABSENCE TO DISCOVERY

1. Holderlin, F. (1961). "Dichterberuf." (The Poet's Vocation). In M. Hamburger, ed., *Selected Verse*. Baltimore: Penguin, p. 138.

2. Partridge, Eric. (1983). *Origins A Short Etymological Dictionary of Modern English*. New York: Greenwich House, p. 554.

3. Moore, Thomas. (1992). *Care of the Soul: A Guide for Cultivating Depth and Sacredness in Everyday Life*. New York: Harper Collins.

4. Emerson, Ralph Waldo. (1965). *The Journals and Miscellaneous Notebooks of Ralph Waldo Emerson*. Merton M. Sealts, ed., Cambridge: Harvard University Press, Vol 5, p. 38.

5. Winnicott, D.W. (1986). *Home is Where We Start From*. New York: W.W. Norton & Company, p. 134.

6. op. cit, p. 266.

7. "The Persistence of Transitional Relatedness." In Paul C. Horton, ed., *The Solace Paradigm: An Eclectic Search for Psychological Immunity.* Madison, CT: International Universities Press, p. 76.

8. Giovacchini, Peter. (1988). *Solace, Structure and Transitional Processes.* In op. cit., Horton, p. 421.

9. Moore, Robert L. (1987). "Ritual Process, Initiation and Contemporary Religion." In Murray Stein and Robert Moore, eds., *Jung's Challenge to Contemporary Religion.* Wilmette, IL: Chiron Publications, p. 155.

10. Corbin, Henry. (1972). "Mundis Imaginalis or the Imaginary and the Imaginal." *Spring.* Dallas: Spring Publications, p. 9.

CHAPTER TWO—FROM DARKNESS TO LIGHT

1. McBride. (1988). "Catholicism and Jungian Psychology." In J. Marvin Spiegelman, Ph.D., ed., *Catholicism and Jungian Psychology.* Phoenix: Falcon Press, p. 187.

2. Jung, C.G. (1967). *Alchemical Studies.* Princeton: Princeton University Press, Bollingen Series XX, p. 37.

3. Jung, C.G. (1971). *Psychological Types.* Princeton: Princeton University Press, Bollingen Series XX, p. 485.

4. Jung, C.G. (1959). *The Archetypes of the Collective Unconscious.* Princeton: Princeton University Press, Bollingen Series XX, p. 4.

5. It is important to note here that the Greek word for soul is psyche, and that psychology is actually "the study of soul."

6. Jacobi, Jolande. (1959). *Complex, Archetype Symbol in the Psychology of C.G. Jung.* Princeton: Princeton University Press, Bollingen Series LVII, pp. 36 & 48.

7. Hopcke, Robert H. (1989). *A Guided Tour of the Collected Works of C.G. Jung.* Boston: Shambhala, p. 15.

8. Lavin, Thomas. (1988). "Hermes: A Guide to the Role of a Priest," In Spiegelman, *Catholicism and Jungian Psychology,* p. 153.

9. McBride, Terrance. (1988). "Catholicism and Jungian Psychology." In Spiegelman, *Catholicism and Jungian Psychology,* p. 184.

10. Jung, C.G. (1953). *Psychology and Alchemy.* Princeton: Princeton University Press, Bollingen Series XX, p. 221.

11. op. cit., Jung, *The Archetypes of the Collective Unconscious,* pp. 37 ff.

12. Ibid., pp. 156-157.

13. Stein, Murray. (1983). *In Midlife.* Dallas: Spring Publications, p. 69.

14. op. cit., Hopcke, p. 16.

15. op. cit., Jung, *The Archetypes and the Collective Unconscious,* p. 8.

16. Jung believed that this prestige was the result of a persona or mask. He said that "one could easily assert that the impelling motive in this development is the will to power. But that would be to forget that the building up of prestige is always the product of collective compromise: not only must there be one who wants prestige, there must also be a public seeking somebody on whom to confer prestige" (*Two Essays on Analytical Psychology*, p. 150). This, it seems, relates directly to the prestige that has traditionally been placed upon priests and that is now waning.

17. Ibid., p. 157.

18. op. cit., Jung, *The Archetypes and the Collective Unconscious*, p. 20.

19. Sipe, A.W.R. (1990). *A Secret World: Sexuality and the Search for Celibacy.* New York: Brunner/Mazel.

20. op. cit., Lavin, p. 152.

21. Bloom, J. (1971). "Who Become Clergymen," *Journal of Religion and Health, 10,* pp. 51 & 53.

22. Dols, William L. (1987). "The Church as Crucible of Transformation." In Murray Stein & Robert Moore, eds., *Jung's Challenge to Contemporary Religion.* Wilmette, IL: Chiron Publications, p. 139.

23. Hillman, James. (1979). *Insearch: Psychology and Religion.* Dallas: Spring Publications, p. 22.

24. Jung, C.G. (1963). *Mysterium Coniunctionis.* Princeton: Princeton University Press, Bollingen Series XX, p. 497.

25. op. cit., Hillman, p. 55.

26. Woodroffe, R.W. (1951). "The Selection of Candidates for the Ministry," *Journal of Pastoral Care, 5,* p. 28.

27. Hillman, James. (1983). *Archetypal Psychology.* Dallas: Spring Publications, p. 39.

28. Kavanaugh, Kieran & Otilio Rodriguez. (trans.) (1964). *The Collected Works of St. John of the Cross.* Washington: ICS Publications, p. 213.

29. Hillman, James. (1990) "Could Psychology Be Part of the Disease, not Part of the Cure?" in Ventura interview, *LA Weekly,* June 1-7, p. 16.

CHAPTER THREE—FROM DEPRESSION TO CONTEMPLATIVE EMPTINESS

1. Heidegger, Martin. (1971). *Poetry, Language, Thought.* New York: Harper/San Francisco, p. 191.

2. Bowers, Margaretta K. (1963). *Conflicts of the Clergy: A Psychodynamic Study With Case Histories.* New York: Thomas Nelson & Sons, p. 13.

3. National Conference of Catholic Bishops, *The Health of American Catholic Priests.* Washington, D.C.: United States Catholic Conference, p. 98.

4. Center for Human Development. (1990). *Formation of Priests: The Challenge of the 1990s.* Washington, D.C.: The Center for Human Development, pp. 15, 24, & 25.

5. Dunn, R.J. (1965). "Personality Patterns Among Religious Personnel: A Review." *Catholic Psychological Record.* 3, p. 134.

6. Kane, Mark J. (1977). *Lions of God, Lambs of God: Psychoanalytic Concepts of Passivity, Dependency and Celibacy within the Christian Clergy.* Oceanside, NY: Dabor Science Publications.

7. cf. Brown & Lowe, *Religious Beliefs and Personality Characteristics of College Students,* 1959; Mitchell, *Priestly Celibacy from a Psychological Perspective,* 1970; Schallert & Kelley, *Some Factors Associated with Voluntary Withdrawal from the Catholic Priesthood,* 1970; Spilka, in Strommen, *Research and Religious Development,* 1971; Strunk, *Interest in the Personality Patterns of Pre-Ministerial Students,* 1959.

8. Vaughn, R.P. (1965). "The Influence of Religious Affiliation on the MMPI Scales." *Journal of Clinical Psychology.* 21, (4), pp. 416-417.

9. Vaughn, R.P. (1962). *Mental Illness and the Religious Life.* Milwaukee: Bruce Publishing Company, p. 130.

10. Jackson, Richard. (1983). "Burnout Among Catholic Priests." *Dissertations Abstract International,* 44, 1595B. (University Microfilms No. 8319168), p. 128.

11. Ibid., p. 178.

12. Ibid., p. 160.

13. Ibid., pp. 223-224.

14. Chiramonte, Anthony José. (1983). "Psychological Correlates of Burnout in Clergymen," *Dissertations Abstract International,* 44, 44/05. (University Microfilms No. MCA83-14854). p. iv.

15. National Conference of Catholic Bishops. (1988). *Reflections on the Morale of Priests.* Washington, D.C.: United States Catholic Conference, p. 9.

16. op. cit., Hillman, *Archetypal Psychology,* p. 42.

17. Jung, C.G. (1953). *Two Essays on Analytical Psychology.* Princeton: Princeton University Press. Bollingen Series XX, p. 52.

18. op. cit., Jung, *Mysterium Coniunctionis,* p. 320.

19. Ibid., p. 497.

20. op. cit., Jung, *Psychology and Alchemy,* p. 36.

21. op. cit., Jung, *Alchemical Studies,* p. 331.

22. Jaffe, Lawrence W. (1990). *Liberating the Heart: Spirituality and Jungian Psychology.* Toronto: Inner City Books, p. 34.

23. Miller, David L. (1989). *Hells and Holy Ghosts.* Nashville: Abingdon Press, p. 27.

24. Wehr, Gerhard. (1985), *Jung: A Biography.* Boston: Shambhala, p. 177.

25. In the Apostolic Constitution on the Rite of Ordination to the Priesthood, we read that an ordained minister is in service as priest, prophet, and king (messiah), in the image of the Christ. *The Rites of the Catholic Church*. (1979). New York: Pueblo Publishing Company. Volume 2, p. 45. For an in-depth analysis of the priesthood in relationship to these roles of priest, prophet, and king, cf. E.O. James, *The Nature and Function of Priesthood*, especially Chapters III, IV, and V.

26. Lockhart, Russell A. (1983). *Words as Eggs*. Dallas: Spring Publications, p. 147.

27. Lockhart, Russell A. (1987). *Psyche Speaks*. Wilimette, IL: Chiron Publications, p. 13-14.

28. In order to use gender neutral language, the word messiah will be employed hereafter rather than the word king, which has traditionally been used in describing priesthood (priest, prophet, king).

29. All quotations from the scriptures will be taken from *The New American Bible*. New York: Thomas Nelson, Inc., 1970.

30. Edinger, Edward. (1985). *Anatomy of the Psyche*. LaSalle, IL: Open Court, p. 38.

31. Ibid., p. 29.

32. Ovid. (1958). *The Metamorphoses*. Horace Greely, (trans.). New York: New American Library, p. 42.

33. Davy, M.M. (1967). *Nicolas Berdyaev*. London: Geoffrey Bles, p. 94.

34. De Waal, Esther. (1989). *Living with Contradiction: Reflections on the Rule of St. Benedict*. San Francisco: Harper & Row, p. 90.

35. Ibid., De Waal, p. 49.

36. Ibid., De Waal, p. 59.

37. McKenzie, John L. (1968). "Aspects of Old Testament Thought," In Raymond Brown, et. al., eds., *The Jerome Biblical Commentary*. Englewood Cliffs, NJ: Prentice-Hall, p. 764.

38. Bruggemann, Walter. (1978). *The Prophetic Imagination*. Philadelphia: Fortress Press, p. 111.

39. Jung, C.G. (1954). *The Development of Personality*. Princeton: Princeton University Press. Bollingen Series XX, pp. 175-176.

40. op. cit., Bruggemann, *The Prophetic Imagination*, p. 46.

41. Becker, Ernest. (1973). *The Denial of Death*. New York: The Free Press, p. 213. This book is a wonderful analysis of the factors that terrorize us concerning death. It offers an insightful understanding of depression as it is related to death.

42. Ibid., Becker, p. 7.

43. Alighieri, Dante. (1954). *The Inferno*. John Ciardi, trans. New York: New American Library, p. 42.

44. op. cit., Bruggemann, *The Prophetic Imagination*, p.111.

45. Michael Crosby correctly defines codependency when he says that it "is in various forms connected to 'external referencing'. Here one's identity is measured by the expectations of others… a kind of mindless adherence to rules and rituals, as well as cultural norms and expectations." Crosby, Michael. (1996). *Celibacy: Means of Control or Mandate of the Heart*. Notre Dame: Ave Maria Press, p. 123.

46. The codependency movement, it seems to me, has contradicted itself by becoming overly authoritarian, encouraging mass conformity to the expectations of these groups. For a good appraisal of this, see Wendy Kraminer. (1992). *I'm Dysfunctional, You're Dysfunctional*. Reading, PA: Addison-Wesley Publishing Company, Inc.

47. op. cit., Partridge, *Origins*, p. 623.

48. Ibid., p. 520.

49. Powers, Jessica. (1984). *The House at Rest*. Pewaukee, WI: Carmelite Monastery, p. 14.

50. op. cit., Kavanaugh, *The Collected Works of John of the Cross*, p. 111.

51. Blackney, Raymond (tr.). *Meister Eckhart: A Modern Translation*. New York: Harper and Row.

52. op. cit., Miller, *Hells and Holy Ghosts*, p. 91.

53. Jung, C.G. (1954). *The Psychology of the Transference*. Princeton: Princeton University Press. Bollinger Series XX, p. 17. Jung was a pioneer in terms of seeing the connections between depression and creativity. cf. *The Harvard Medical School Mental Health Letter*, Vol. 6, No. 7, December 1990, p. 6 and June 1985, pp. 4-6.

54. *Eckhart, Meister*. (1981). Edmund Colledge & Bernard McGinn (tr.), *The Classics of Western Spirituality*. New York: Paulist Press, p. 248.

CHAPTER FOUR—FROM BEING PERFECT TO LIVING WITH IMPERFECTION

1. Rich, Adrienne. (1983). Quoted in Matthew Fox, *Original Blessing*. Santa Fe: Bear and Company, p. 110.

2. For a full description of perfectionism see the articles by David A. Burns. (1980). "The Perfectionist's Script for Self-Defeat." *Psychology Today*, November, pp. 34-52; and Asher R. Pacht. (1984). "Reflections on Perfection." *American Psychologist*, April, Vol 39, No. 4, pp. 386-390.

3. op. cit., Burns. (1980). p. 50.

4. Samuels, Andrew. (1989). *Plural Psyche*. London: Routledge, pp. 199-200.

5. op. cit., Burns. (1980). p. 46.

6. Graham, John R. (1987). *The MMPI*. New York: Oxford University Press, pp. 59-60.

7. Arnold, Magda, et.al. (1962). *Screening Candidates for Priesthood and Religious Life*. Chicago: Loyola University Press, p. 73.

8. Rice, P.J. (1958). *An MMPI Study of Religious Seminarians.* Unpublished Master's Thesis, Loyola University of Chicago, p. 62.

9. W. C. Bier, (1956) found seminarians and priests to be high on Scale 7 (psychasthenia) of the MMPI. Richard Vaughn, (1963, 1970) states that seminarians are high in psychasthenia and that they tend to be perfectionistic and scrupulous. The research of James Dittes (1962) also indicates that seminarians are high on Scale 7 (psychasthenia) of the MMPI. Robert Sweeny, (1964) in his study of 461 seminarians, found them to be high on this scale of the MMPI. Ralph Dunn, (1965) in his MMPI studies, discovered that seminarians are high in psychasthenia and that they tend to be perfectionistic, worrisome, and self-conscious. In his MMPI analysis of 99 seminarians, John Grant (1967) found the mean T-score for the entire group on Scale 7 to be around 65, which is 1 1/2 standard deviations above the mean of 50 for the MMPI.

10. Newlon, Nancy & Eric Mansager. (1986). "Adlerian Lifestyles Among Catholic Priests." *Individual Psychology Journal of Adlerian Theory*, 42, (3), p. 372.

11. Natale, S. (1982). "Dynamics in Religious Organizations which Induce Stress," *Journal of Pastoral Care*, 17, pp. 57-58.

12. op. cit., National Conference of Catholic Bishops, *Health Care...*, p. 98.

13. Ibid., p. 39.

14. op. cit., Center for Human Development. (1990), pp. 15, 19, 20, 25.

15. Ibid., p. 19.

16. This psychopathology will be discussed in much greater detail in a later chapter since it is essential to the understanding of archetypal patterns in the priesthood. Passive-aggression is described by the *Diagnostic and Statistical Manual of Mental Disorders, III*—Revised in people who "are passively expressing covert aggression," p. 356.

17. The institutional church tends to have excessive control over the lives of priests; this powerful dominance can actually help in creating passive-aggressive responses. Perhaps it would be better for the hierarchical church to move beyond its current control over every aspect of priestly life and ministry to allow greater independence for its priests and brothers. This adjustment toward greater freedom could invite more people to its priestly and religious ranks and also impact the church in terms of the many current legal and civil lawsuits which are pending in reference to priests and brothers. Since the hierarchical church assumes responsibility for every aspect of the life and work of its ordained ministers and religious brothers, it is also responsible for any legal or civil actions that are taken against any of these individuals. Greater independence for priests and brothers might decrease psychological problems such as depression, perfectionism, and passive-aggressive sexual acting out, and could also lessen these traumatic legal problems for the institutional church as a whole. (cf. Perri, W.D. [1992]. *A Multivariant Analysis of Psychologically Evaluated Roman Catholic Priests and Brothers: Comparisons of Psychological Symptomatology, Sexual Orientation and Age.)*

18. op. cit., Burns. (1980). p. 38.

19. op. cit., Pacht. (1984). *Reflections on Perfection,* p. 387.

20. Slade, et. al. (1991). "An Experimental Analysis of Perfectionism and Dissatisfaction." *British Journal of Clinical Psychology,* May, Vol 30 (2), pp. 169-176.

21. op. cit., Pacht, p. 389.

22. op. cit., McKenzie. (1968). "The Gospel According to Matthew." In *The Jerome Biblical Commentary*, p. 73.

23. Carter, Sydney. (1982). *Dance in the Dark*. New York: Crossroad, p. 30.

24. Guggenbuhl-Craig, Adolf. (1980). *Eros on Crutches*. Dallas: Spring Publications, p. 15.

25. Sabourin, Leopold. (1973). *Priesthood: A Comparative Study*. Leiden, Belgium: E. J. Brill, p. 9.

26. James, E. O. (1955). *The Nature and Function of Priesthood*. New York: Barnes and Noble, p. 32.

27. op. cit. Guggenbuhl-Craig, (1980), pp. 21-25.

28. Ibid., p. 25.

29. For a good discussion of this see Andrew Samuels. (1985). *Jung and the Post-Jungians*. London: Routledge & Kegan Paul, pp. 108-111.

30. A footnote to this passage in the New American Bible says that there is not an intention here to reject authority, but authoritarianism, and the failure to acknowledge that authority exists to serve.

31. op. cit. Samuels. (1989). *Plural Psyche*, p. 8.

32. Ibid., Samuels, p. 194.

33. op. cit., Kavanaugh. (1973). *The Collected Works of John of the Cross*, p. 326.

34. Bishop, Peter. (1986). "The Shadow of the Holistic Earth." Dallas: Spring Publications, p. 63.

35. op. cit., De Waal. (1989). *Living with Contradiction*, pp. 12-13.

36. op. cit. Osborne, p. 23.

CHAPTER FIVE—FROM ABUSIVE POWER TO INTIMACY

1. op. cit., Guggenbuhl-Craig. (1980). *Eros on Crutches: On the Nature of the Psychopath*, p. 80.

2. op. cit., Osborne. (1988). *Priesthood: A History of the Ordained Ministry in the Roman Catholic Church*, pp. 79-80.

3. op. cit., James. (1955). *The Nature and Function of Priesthood*, p. 107.

4. op. cit., Sabourin. (1973). *Priesthood: A Comparative Study*, pp. 6-7.

5. Ibid., p. 84.

6. Bier, W. C. (1956). "A Comparative Study of Five Catholic College Groups on the MMPI," In G. S. Walsh & W. G. Dohlstrom, (eds.), *Basic Readings on the MMPI in Psychology and Medicine*. Minneapolis, MN: University of Minnesota Press, p. 607.

7. op. cit. Arnold, Hispanicus, Weisgerber, et. al. *Screening Candidates for Priesthood and Religious Life,* p. 121.

8. Ibid., p. 96.

9. Wauck, Leroy. (1956). *An Investigation of the Usefulness of Psychological Tests in the Selection of Candidates for the Diocesan Priesthood*. Unpublished Doctoral Dissertation, Loyola University of Chicago, p. 127.

10. Ibid., p. 127.

11. Grant, John G. (1967). *A Study of Deliberate Faking in the MMPI with Seminarians*. Unpublished Doctoral Dissertation, Loyola University of Chicago, p. 78.

12. Weisgerber, C. (1969). *Psychological Assessment of Candidates for Religious Orders*. Chicago: Loyola University Press, p. 67.

13. Ibid., p. 70.

14. op. cit., Rice, *An MMPI Study of Religious Seminarians*, p. 70.

15. McAllister, R. J. & A. VanderVeldt. (1965). "Psychiatric Illness in Hospitalized Catholic Religious," *American Journal of Psychiatry*, 121, p. 884.

16. McAllister, R. J. (1965). "The Emotional Health of the Clergy," *Journal of Religion and Health*, 4, p. 334.

17. Barry, W. A. & E. S. Bordin. (1967). "Personality Development and the Vocation Choice of the Ministry," *Journal of Counseling Psychology*, 14, pp. 395-403.

18. op. cit., Center for Human Development, *Formation of Priests: The Challenge of the 1990s*.

19. op. cit., In Strommen, *Research on Religious Development*, p. 430 ff.

20. Greeley, Andrew & R. R. Schoenerr. (1972). *The Catholic Priest in the United States: Sociological Investigations*. Washington, DC: United States Catholic Conference, p. 133 ff.

21. Hall, Douglas T. & Benjamin Schneider. (1973). *Organizational Climates and Careers: The Work Lives of Priests*. New York: Seminar Press, p. 108.

22. Rulla & Maddi, (1972) *Personality and the Catholic Religious Vocation: Self and Conflict in Male Entrants*, "The orientation of deference, of submissiveness, of obedience present in values like "doing my duty" and "having fine relations with other people" may be the defensive reaction formation against a strongly repressed, unacceptable orientation of rebelliousness, aggressive autonomy or it may be based on a conflictual trend to conforming symbiosis." p. 71. Also, see Rulla, et. al., (1979). *Psychological Structure and Vocation*, and Rulla, et. al., (1976). *Entering and Leaving Vocation: Intrapsychic Dynamics*.

23. cf., Bloom, (1971). *Who Become Clergymen*; Kobler, (1964). *Screening Applicants for Religious Life*; Whitlock, (1959). *The Relationship Between Passivity of Personality and Personal Factors Related to the Choice of the Ministry as a Vocation.*

24. Christensen, Carl W. (1966). "The Occurrence of Mental Illness in the Clergy: Personality Disorders," *The Journal of Pastoral Care*, 17, p. 133.

25. op. cit., Mitchell. (1970). p. 222.

26. op. cit., McAllister & VanderVeldt. (1965). p. 882.

27. op. cit. Mitchell, p. 221.

28. op. cit. Crosby. (1996).

29. op. cit., National Conference of Catholic Bishops. (1988). "Reflections on the Morale of Priests."

30. op. cit., Nelson, (1989). "Psychological Correlates of Adjustment in Roman Catholic Priests." p. 51.

31. Loftus, Robert J. (1973). "The Difference Between Priests Legally and Personally Committed to Celibacy," Unpublished Doctoral Dissertation: University of Notre Dame, p. 5496-A.

32. Crosby, Michael H. (1991). *The Dysfunctional Church*. Notre Dame: Ave Maria Press, p. 109. This book is very helpful in terms of understanding authentic leadership in the church and how this leadership has gone awry. Crosby uses the Gospel of Matthew to fortify his arguments.

33. Wolman, Benjamin. (1987). *The Sociopathic Personality*. New York: Brunner/Mazel, p. 159.

34. Hesselbrock, M. N., et. al. (1985). "Psychopathology in Hospitalized Alcoholics," *Archives of General Psychiatry*, 42: 1050-1055. Rounsaville, B. (June, 1988). "Executive Summary: Psychiatric Comorbidity in Alcoholics." Unpublished paper prepared for the IOM Committee for the Study of Treatment and Rehabilitation Services for Alcoholism and Alcohol Abuse.

35. This is a disorder called alexithymia where people develop a particular inability to express their feelings.

36. Kelsey, Morton. (1988). "Rediscovering the Priesthood through the Unconscious." In Robert L. Moore, ed., *Carl Jung and Christian Spirituality*, p. 135.

37. Mohandas Ghandi is an example of this.

38. op. cit., The Center for Human Development. (1990). *The Challenge of the 1990s: Formation of Priests*, p. 26. This document goes to great lengths to connect psychosexual maturity with authentic leadership abilities. Sadly, the Synod of Bishops seems to have paid very little attention to its recommendations.

39. Schelke, Karl. (1969). "Ministry and Minister in the New Testament Church." In Rahner, Karl (ed.). "The Identity of the Priest," *Concilium*, Vol 43, New York: Paulist Press.

40. Ibid., Schelkle. (1969). p. 18.

41. Abbott, Walter. (ed.). (1966). *The Documents of Vatican II.* New York: Catholic Book Publishing Company, pp. 538-546.

42. Ibid., *The Documents of Vatican II,* pp. 546 ff. Many articles in this regard have also been written in the past 30 years. cf. Peter Cantwell, O.F.M., Ph.D. "Ongoing Growth Through Intimacy," in *Human Development,* Vol. 2, Number 3, Fall, 1981. Mary Kenel, Ph.D., "A Celibate's Sexuality and Intimacy," in *Human Development,* Vol. 7, Number i, Spring, 1986. *A Reflection Guide on Human Sexuality and the Ordained Priesthood.* U.S. Bishops' Committee on Priestly Life and Ministry, 1983. Susanne Breckel, R.S.M., Ph.D., N. Michael Murphy, Ph.D. "Psychosexual Development." *Chicago Studies,* Vol. 20. Number 1, Spring 1981. Michael Garanzini, S. J. "Psychodynamic Theory and Pastoral Theology: An Integrated Model" in *Homosexuality and Religion.* The Haworth Press, 1989. Donna T. Mahoney. *Touching the Face of God: Intimacy and Celibacy in Priestly Life.* Jeremiah Press, 1991. John Struzzo, Ph.D. "Intimate Relationships: Heterosexual and Homosexual." *Relationships.* pp. 91-111.

43. Guggenbuhl-Craig, Adolf. (1971). *Power in the Helping Professions.* Dallas: Spring Publications, p. 23.

44. op. cit., Guggenbuhl-Craig, *Eros on Crutches,* pp. 84 & 106-109.

45. Berry, Patricia. (1982). *Echo's Subtle Body.* Dallas: Spring Publications, p. 4.

46. op. cit., Samuels. (1989). *Plural Psyche,* p. 208.

47. Kennedy, Eugene, et. al. (1972). *The Catholic Priest in the United States: Psychological Investigations.* Washington, DC: United States Catholic Conference, p. 80.

Chapter Six—From Stereotypes to Role Flexibility

1. Poncé, Charles (1988). *Working the Soul.* Berkeley: North Atlantic Books.

2. This is not the place for a long discussion of this issue in our culture. For a better understanding of gender role versus gender identity issues the reader is referred to the following books and articles: *The Psychology of Sex Differences,* by E. E. Maccoby and C. N. Jacklin. (1974). Stanford, CA: Stanford University Press: *Androgyny* by June Singer. (1977). Anchor Books. *The Forty-Nine Percent Majority: The Male Sex Role,* by Deborah David and Robert Brannon, (eds.). (1976). Addison-Wesley Publishing Co. and *Sex Roles and Human Behavior* by Kay Schaffer (1981). Winthrop Publishers, Inc. *The Psychology of Sex Differences* by Hilary Lips and Nina Lee Colwill (1978), Englewood Cliffs, NJ: Prentice-Hall, Inc. *American Psychologist,* Volume 50, Number 3, March 1995. Cook, Ellen P. (1985). *Psychological Androgyny.* New York: Pergamon Books. Gilmore, David D. (1990). *Manhood in the Making.* New Haven: Yale University Press.

3. Eagly, Alice H. "The Science and Politics of Comparing Men and Women," in *American Psychologist,* Volume 50, Number 3, March 1995, p. 154.

4. Graham, John R. (1987). *The MMPI: A Practical Guide.* Oxford: Oxford University Press, p. 51.

5. Masters, William, Virginia Johnson & Robert Kolodny (1992). *Human Sexuality*. New York: Harper Collins, p. 277.

6. cf., Skrinkowski, 1952, pp. 35–37; op. cit., Rice, 1958, p. 60; Dittes, 1962, p. 153; Murphy, 1962, p. 23; Vaughn, 1963, p. 66; Sweeny, 1964, p. 63; op. cit., Grant, 1967, pp. 73 & 84; op. cit., Weisgerber, 1969, p. 155.

7. op. cit., Bier. (1948). *A Comparative Study of a Seminary Group with Four Other Groups on the MMPI*, p. 91. "The greatest inter-group differences for the seminary group were found in the Mf (interest) scale, where ten out of twelve differences reached significance at the .01 per cent level."

8. op. cit., Bier. (1956). "A Comparative Study of Five Catholic College Groups on the MMPI." In Welsh & Dohlstrom, (eds.). *Basic Readings on the MMPI in Psychology and Medicine*, p. 598. "The Mf scale is the one on which the seminary group manifests the most divergence from the general test norms and the scores of the other groups."

9. op. cit., Barry & E. S. Bordin. (1967). *Personality Development and the Vocation Choice of the Ministry*, p. 398.

10. op. cit., Arnold, et. al. (1962). *Screening Candidates for Priesthood and Religious Life*, p. 121.

11. op. cit., Dunn. (1965). *Personality Patterns Among Religious Personnel*, p. 133.

12. Jansen, D. G. & F. J. Garvey. (1973). "High-Average and Low Rated Clergymen in a State Hospital Clinical Program," *Journal of Clinical Psychology*, 29, pp. 89–92.

13. op. cit., Kobler. (1964). *Screening Applicants for the Religious Life*, p. 165.

14. op. cit., National Conference of Catholic Bishops. (1988). *Reflections on the Morale of Priests*, p. 8.

15. Closely related to the cognitive processes the priest invokes to handle stress is the concept of learned helplessness. Here the church system may function to further the depression in the form of helplessness and powerlessness (Abramson, Seligman & Teasdale, 1978). The system has fostered a dependency among priests... This dependency may work to prevent the priest from taking active steps to reduce his stressful situation... Future research might investigate the role of power among priests and the church, particularly its relationship to self-esteem, depression and burn-out. op. cit., Jackson. (1983). *Burnout Among Catholic Priests*, pp. 180–181.

16. op. cit., Strommen (ed.). (1971). *Research on Religious Development*, p. 455. On the scale in which seminarians notoriously show the peak score (Mf), Cardwell (1967) has given the most careful appraisal yet. She reports the scores of her sample on various subscales, and she finds that the largest component of the Mf score comes from the altruism subscale, the smallest component from the strictly sexual identification.

17. op. cit., Kane (1977) reviewed the literature in his psychoanalytic analysis of priests and religious men entitled *Lions of God, Lambs of God: Psychoanalytic Concepts of Passivity, Dependency and Celibacy Within the Christian Clergy* and states: Lee (1962) studied characteristic patterns of Catholic seminarians and

ex-seminarians, labeling them "persisters" and "leavers" respectively...
Submissiveness, femininity, conformity, and unquestioning adherence to the
authority of the church are discriminatory characteristics between persisters
and leavers and are predominant personality variables of those who remain in
the seminary... Lee finds the persisters to be submissive, group dependent,
sociable, friendly, more feminine in interests than the leavers... Lee's findings
regarding submissiveness are supported by McCarthy (1942) who studied 85
Catholic major seminarians and 144 concluded that high femininity scores
seemed to be a clergy trademark.

18. Thomas, Gordon. (1986). *Desire and Denial: Celibacy and the Church*. Boston:
Little, Brown and Company, p. 9.

19. op. cit., Cook, *Psychological Androgyny*, 1985.

20. Keller, Catherine. (1986). *From a Broken Web*. Boston: Beacon Press, p. 86.

21. op. cit., Poncé, p. 116.

22. Teilhard de Chardin, Pierre. (1957). *The Divine Milieu*. New York: Harper
and Row, p. 80.

23. Bouyer, Louis. (1982). *The Spirituality of the New Testament and the Fathers*.
New York: The Seabury Press, p. 145.

24. Neumann, Erich. (1954). *The Origins and History of Consciousness*. Princeton:
Princeton University Press. Bollingen Series XLII, p. 157.

25. op. cit., James. (1955). *The Nature and Function of Priesthood*, p. 15. An her-
maphrodite is actually a plant, animal, or person who possesses both male and
female reproductive organs. It seems that he actually means androgyny.

26. Monick, Eugene. (1987). *Phallos*. Toronto: Inner City Books, p. 70.

27. *The Revelations of Divine Love of Julian of Norwich* (1974). James Walsh, trans.
St. Meinrad, IN: Abbey Press, p. 166.

28. op. cit., Esther De Waal. (1989). *Living With Contradictions*. p. 19.

29. op. cit., Jung. (1963). *Mysterium Coniunctionis*, pp. 373–374.

30. Ibid., p. 422.

31. op. cit., Poncé. (1988). *Working the Soul*, p. 75.

32. cf. Randy P. Conner. (1993). *Blossom of Bone*. San Francisco: Harper Collins.

33. Eliade, Mircea. (1964). *Shamanism*. Princeton: Princeton University Press.
Bollingen Series LXXVI, p. 395. See also, pp. 125 (note), 257–258, 351–353, 461.

34. Roscoe, Will. (1991). *The Zuni Man-Woman*. Albuquerque: The University of
New Mexico Press, p. 2.

35. Ibid., p. 167.

36. Hopcke, Robert. (1989). *Jung, Jungians and Homosexuality*. Boston:
Shambhala, p. 182.

37. Hultkrantz, Ake. (1989). "Health, Religion and Medicine in Native

American Traditions," in Lawrence Sullivan, *Healing and Restoring: Health and Medicine in the World's Religious Traditions.* New York: Macmillan Publishing Company, pp. 327–358.

38. op. cit., Roscoe, pp. 18, 22, 25, 146, 165.

39. op. cit., Hillman. (1979). *Insearch,* p. 107.

40. Ziegler, Alfred J. (1983). *Archetypal Medicine.* Dallas: Spring Publications, p. 45.

41. op. cit., Lavin. (1988). p. 157.

42. op. cit., Jaffe. (1990). p. 38.

43. op. cit., Jung. (1963). *Mysterium Coniunctionis,* p. 90. For a description of this androgynous state in the Judeo-Christian creation story see Robert Graves & Raphael Patai. (1963). *Hebrew Myths.* New York: Anchor Books, pp. 66–67.

44. Corbett, Lionel. (1987). "Transformation of the Image of God Leading to Self-Initiation in Old Age." In: *Betwixt & Between: Patterns of Masculine and Feminine Initiation,* L. Mahdi, S. Foster & M. Little (eds.). LaSalle, IL: Open Court, pp. 376–382.

45. Gallagher, Charles & Thomas Vandenberg (1987). *The Celibacy Myth.* New York: Crossroad, p. 94.

46. op. cit., Perri. (1992).

47. Duckworth, J & W. Anderson. (1986). *MMPI Interpretation Manual for Counselors and Clinicians.* Muncie, IN: Accelerated Development, Inc., Publishers, p. 163.

48. op. cit., Johnson, et. al. (1992). *Human Sexuality,* p. 278.

49. As Tom Lavin suggests in his article, "Hermes: A Guide to the Role of the Priest," this is related to the mercurial nature of priesthood .For more information see: Spiegelman, ed. *Catholicism and Jungian Psychology,* pp. 160 ff.

50. op. cit., Keller. (1986), p. 228.

51. op. cit., Poncé. (1988). *Working the Soul,* p. 70.

52. op. cit. *The Rites of the Catholic Church.* (1979). Volume Two, p. 66.

53. op. cit., Becker. (1973). *The Denial of Death,* p. 11.

CHAPTER SEVEN—PASSIVE-AGGRESSION TO LIVING THE CHAOS

1. op. cit., Dols, p. 142.

2. op. cit., Greeley. (1972). *The Catholic Priest in the United States; Sociological Investigations,* pp. 43-44. ...The tendency to be passive-aggressive, that is to say, to control people not so much by self-assertion as by being a "nice guy," is not especially surprising considering the fact that the priestly role until recently was one in which a man had many and serious responsibilities with rather little authority and independence to meet them... When the passive-aggressive personality begins to assert his aggressiveness overtly, he is likely to exagger-

ate considerably the cathartic behavior, and of course he has a lot of past aggressions to release, aggressions toward his superiors and teachers from the past as well as those from his childhood that he has never properly faced. One wonders how much of the conflict in the present milieu of American Catholicism is a part of the painful process of "nice guys" trying to become effective militants. pp. 47-48.

3. op. cit., Weisgerber. (1969). "Psychological Assessment of Candidates for Religious Orders," p. 123. Weisgerber found that 37% of his sample of seminarians had 45/54 configurations on the MMPI. Of these, about 68% persevered to ordination. Banks, Stephen, et. al. (1984). "Progress in the Evaluation and Prediction of Successful Candidates for Religious Careers." *Counseling and Values*, Vol 28 (2), pp. 82-91. Banks and his collaborators, plus William Bier, S. J., in both of his studies, found seminarians to be high on both scales 4 and 5 of the MMPI. Sweeny, R. H. (1964). "Testing Seminarians on the MMPI and the Kuder: A Report on Ten Years of Testing," p. 63. Sweeny, in his analysis of 461 seminarians, found that the highest scale on the MMPI was Mf and that Pd was in the next three highest scales. Grant, J. (1967). "A Study of Deliberate Faking in the MMPI with Seminarians." p. 63. Grant found similar results in his probe of 99 seminarians.

4. Graham, J. R. (1977). *The MMPI: A Practical Guide.* New York: Oxford University Press, pp. 72-73.

5. op. cit., Duckworth & Anderson. (1987). *MMPI Interpretation Manual for Counselors and Clinicians.* p. 171. "Males with this configuration may have a passive-aggressive personality... The 5-4 combination is a common configuration for men who are nonconformists. They seem to delight in defying social conventions in their behavior and dress."

6. op. cit., Arnold, et. al. (1962). *Screening Candidates for Priesthood and Religious Life*, p. 117. Arnold and her colleagues found that seminarians are high on both Scale 4 and Scale 5 in the MMPI. Of the 139 candidates in their study who persevered to ordination, the mean T-score on the Pd scale was 62.64. For this same group, the mean T-score for the MF scale was 67.66. For the 69 candidates who left the seminary prior to being ordained, the mean T-score for Pd was 63.60 and the mean T-score for Mf was 68.48. All of these scores are well above one standard deviation from the mean. This suggests some inclination toward passive-aggressive tendencies in these subjects.

7. op. cit., Dunn. (1965). "Personality Patterns Among Religious Personnel: A Review." p. 135.

8. op. cit., Whitlock. (1959). "The Relationship Between Passivity of Personality and Personal Factors Related to the Choice of the Ministry as a Vocation." p. 113.

9. op. cit., Center for Human Development. (1990). *Formation of Priests: The Challenge of the 1990s*, pp. 15ff.

10. op. cit., Strommen. (1971). *Research on Religious Development*, pp. 422ff.

11. op. cit., Kane. (1972). "A Comparison of the Degree of Passive-Receptiveness Between Roman Catholic and Protestant Clergymen." pp. 34-36.

12. op. cit., McAllister & VanderVeldt, (1965). "Psychiatric Illness in Hospitalized Catholic Religious." p. 882.

13. op. cit., Thomas. (1986). *Desire and Denial: Celibacy and the Church.* p. 10.

14. Rulla, L. M. (1972). "Personality and the Catholic Religious Vocation: Self and Conflict in Male Entrants." *Journal of Personality*, Vol. 40 (4), pp. 564-587. Rulla describes seminarians as having problems with power, being narcissistic, dependent, rebellious, aggressive, masochistic, compliant, having high adaptability and succorance needs coupled with elevated needs for dominance and aggression. J. O. Meany speaks of priests as having symptoms which are indicative of dependency and authority. cf. Meany. (1972-1973). "Psychological Struggle with Dependency in Current Catholicism." *The Journal of Pastoral Counseling*, Vol 7 (2), pp. 17-23.

15. Sammon, S. D., et.al. (1985). "Psychosocial Development and Stressful Life Events Among Religious Professionals," *Journal of Personality and Social Psychology*, 48, (3), pp. 680ff.

16. op. cit., Schallert and Kelley. (1970). "Some Factors Associated with Voluntary Withdrawal from the Catholic Priesthood." pp. 447ff.

17. op. cit., Strommen. (1971). pp. 469-470. Bernard Spilka and Paul Werme note that seminarians have conflicts with aggression, insecurity, and that they tend to withdraw in times of personal conflict. op. cit., Christensen. (1966). "The Occurrence of Mental Illness in the Clergy: Personality Disorders." p. 126. Christensen studied 51 clergymen with personality disorders and found that 20 of the 51, or 39%, were passive-aggressive. op. cit., Barry & Bordin. (1967). "Personality Development and the Vocation Choice of the Ministry." p. 398. These authors describe inferiority coupled with a need for dominance in men who enter the ministry. They accurately characterize the conflict between dominance and passivity that is found in much of the related literature.

18. op. cit., Barry and Bordin. (1967). "Personality Development and the Vocation Choice of the Ministry." p. 398.

19. Marmar, Charles R. (1988). "Personality Disorders." In Howard Goldmann, ed., *Review of General Psychiatry.* Norwalk, CT: Appleton & Lange, p. 421.

20. Gunderson, John G. (1988). "Personality Disorders." In Armand Nicholi, ed., *The New Harvard Guide to Psychiatry.* Cambridge, MA: Harvard University Press, p. 354.

21. Mahrer, Alvin R. (1983). "An Existential-Experiential View and Operational Perspective on Passive-Aggressiveness." In Richard Parsons and Robert Wicks, ed., *Passive-Aggressiveness.* New York: Brunner/Mazel, p. 105. "An understanding of these traits is enhanced by seeing them in their childhood development: The child starts with a deeper potential for experiencing power and control, but in a way which is painful and unpleasant. In order for this experiencing to occur, the child may become a passively controlling person who believes in helpless and needy ways which both secure and aggressively control some external victim. Therefore, the person gains a measure of the deeper experience of power and control.

22. For an analysis of this see: op. cit., Perri. (1992).

23. op. cit., Mahrer. (1983). p. 213.

24. Breger, Louis. (1974). *From Instinct to Identity.* Englewood Cliffs, NJ: Prentice-Hall, p. 47.

25. Ibid., p. 350.

26. See the lives of John of the Cross, Thomas Aquinas, Catherine of Siena, Teresa of Avila, Teilhard de Chardin, Meister Eckhart, etc.

27. Ibid., Breger, p. 351.

28. Midgley, Mary. (1978). *Beast and Man.* Ithaca, NY: Cornell University Press, p. 81.

29. A good friend of mine believes that all of the lawsuits that the church has had to face recently regarding priests who have abused minors is partly a result of pent-up rage at authority. For the first time, people have been able to break through the rigid hierarchical walls and confront the inflexible power structures.

30. "Fear is useless. What is needed is trust" (Mark 5: 36). "Do not fear those who deprive the body of life but cannot destroy the soul" (Matthew 10:28). "In very truth, even the hairs of your head are counted! Fear nothing, then. You are worth more than a flock of sparrows" (Luke 12:7). "You did not receive a spirit of slavery leading you back to fear, but a spirit of adoption through which we cry out, Abba!" (Romans 8:15).

31. op. cit., Breger. (1974). p. 233.

32. Fromm, Erich. (1976). *To Have Or To Be.* New York: Bantam Books, pp. 30 & 68.

33. op. cit., Wicks, pp. 218-220.

34. op. cit., Fromm, p. 66.

35. op. cit., Fromm, p. 93.

36. op. cit., Fromm, p. 53.

37. op. cit., Fromm, p. 77.

38. Watkins, Mary. (1984). *Waking Dream.* Dallas: Spring Publications, cf. p. 104.

39. op. cit., Hampden-Turner. (1981). pp. 28-29.

40. Millon, Theodore. (1981). *Disorders of Personality.* New York: John Wiley and Sons, p. 253.

CHAPTER EIGHT—FROM CONTRADICTION TO AMBIVALENCE

1. Jung, C. G. *The Vision Seminars,* p. 206.

2. op. cit., Jung. (1959). *The Archetypes of the Collective Unconscious,* pp. 37 ff.

3. Ibid., p. 15.

4. op. cit., Millon. (1981). p. 258. Millon states that this style is not a failure because it is an ingenious way of getting a reward. Perhaps the reward is to be found right here in the illness itself, and the bonus is God's gift of rediscovering the indelible mark of priesthood.

5. op. cit., Midgley. (1978). p. 47.

6. Carotenuto, Aldo. (1989). *Eros and Pathos*. Toronto: Inner City Books, p. 95.

7. op. cit., Midgley, p. 341.

8. op. cit., Dols, pp. 142-143.

9. op. cit., De Waal, p. 11.

10. op. cit., Teilhard de Chardin, p. 89.

11. Ibid., Teilhard de Chardin, p. 89.

12. op. cit., De Waal, p. 23.

CHAPTER NINE—AN INITIATION RITE

1. op. cit., Becker, *The Denial of Death*, p. 69.

2. Cirlot, J. E. (1962). *A Dictionary of Symbols*. New York: Philosophical Library, p. 147.

3. op. cit., Hampden-Turner, p. 155.

4. Romanyshyn, Robert D. (1982). *Psychological Life: From Science to Metaphor*.

5. Quoting McGratty on The Sacred Heart. Austin, TX: University of Texas Press, p. 129.

6. op. cit., Ziegler, p. 88.

7. DeMarco, Robert. (1992). "The Heart of Jesus in a Cordless World." *Homiletic and Pastoral Review*, January, Vol XCII, (4), p. 51.

8. op. cit., Romanyshyn, p. 103.

9. op. cit., Ziegler, p. 95.

10. James. (1958). *Varieties of Religious Experience*, p. 121.

11. op. cit., Romanyshyn, p. 119.

12. op. cit., DeMarco, p. 54.

13. op. cit., Dols. p. 143.

14. Maslow, Abraham. (1964). *Religions, Values and Peak Experiences*. New York: The Viking Press, p. 12.

15. Ibid. Maslow. (1964). pp. 12-14.

16. Sinetar, Marsha. (1986). *Ordinary People as Monks and Mystics*. New York: Paulist Press, p. 5.

17. Rilke, Rainer Maria. (1978). *Duino Elegies.* David Young (trans.). New York: W. W. Norton & Company, p. 48.

18. Miller, David L. (1980). "Theology's Ego/Religion's Soul." *Spring.* Dallas: Spring Publications, p. 82.

19. op. cit., Keller. (1986). p. 91.

20. Tillich, Paul. *The Shaking of the Foundations.* New York: Charles Scribner's Sons, p. 163.

21. Bly, Robert. (1988). *A Little Book on the Human Shadow.* San Francisco: Harper and Row, p. 53ff.

22. op. cit., Partridge. (1983). p. 681.

23. op. cit., Jung. (1977). *Mysterium Coniunctionis,* p. 364.

24. op. cit., T. S. Eliot, "East Cocker." p. 186.

25. Larsen, Stephen. (1990). *The Mythic Imagination.* New York: Bantam Books, p. 127.

26. Fox, Matthew. (1990). *Breakthrough: Meister Eckhart's Creation Spirituality in New Translation.* New York: Image Books, p. 162.

27. op. cit., Miller. (1989), p. 92.

Bibliography

Collins, Pat. (1995). *Intimacy and the Hungers of the Heart*. Mystic, CT: Twenty-Third Publications.

Dols, William L. (1987). The church as crucible of transformation. In Murray Stein & Robert Moore, (eds.), *Jung's Challenge to Contemporary Religion*. Wilmette IL: Chiron Publications, Inc.

Fox, Thomas C. (1995) *Sexuality and Catholicism*. New York: George Braziller.

Frazee, Charles A. (1972). The origins of clerical celibacy in the western church. *Church History*, 41 (2), 149-167.

Griffin, David Ray. (1989). *Archetypal Process*. Evanston, IL: Northwestern University Press.

Hammond, Philip E., Salinas, Luis and Sloane, Douglas. (1978). Types of clergy authority: Their measurement, location and effects. *Journal for the Scientific Study of Religion*, 17 (3), 241-253.

Hemrick, Eugene and Hoge, Dean R. (1985). *Seminarians in theology: A national profile*. Washington, D.C.: United States Catholic Conference.

Hoge, Dean R., Potvin, Raymond H. & Ferry, Kathleen M. (1984). *Research on men's vocations to the priesthood and religious life*. Washington, D.C.: United States Catholic Conference.

Holmes, Urban T, III. (1974). The feminine priestly symbol and the meaning of God. *St. Luke's Journal of Theology*, 17, 3-22.

Komonchak, Joseph A.   (1981).   Celibacy and tradition. *Chicago Studies: Sexuality and the Priesthood*, 20, (1), Spring, 5-18.

Mahoney, Donna Tiernan. (1991). *Touching the Face of God: Intimacy and Celibacy in Priestly Life*. Boca Raton: FL: Jeremiah Press.

Meloy, J. Reid. (1986). Narcissistic psychopathology and the clergy. *Pastoral Psychology*, 35, 50-55.

Miller, David L. (1980). Theology's ego/religion's soul. *Spring*. Dallas: Spring Publications.

Mitchell, K.R.   (1970).   Priestly celibacy from a psychological perspective. *Journal of Pastoral Care*, 24 (4), 564-587.

Moore, T.V. (1936). Insanity in priests and religious: I: The rate of insanity in priests and religious; II: The detection of prepsychotics who apply for admission to the priesthood and religious communities. *American Ecclesiastical Review*, 95, 485-498, 601-613.

Morgan, Edward. (1980). Implications of the masculine and the feminine in the pastoral ministry. *Journal of Pastoral Care*, 34, 268-277.

National Conference of Catholic Bishops. (1977). *Human sexuality and the ordained priesthood*. Washington, D.C.: United States Catholic Conference.

National Federation of Priests' Councils. (1991). *Consultation on priests' morale: A review of research*. Chicago: NFPC Publication.

Nelson, Daniel C.   (1989).   Psychological correlates of adjustment in Roman Catholic priests.   *Dissertation Abstracts International*, 50, 3170B. (University Microfilms No. 8925429).

O'Kane, Francoise. (1994). *Sacred Chaos: Reflections on God's Shadow and the Dark Self*. Toronto: Inner City Books.

O'Neill, David P. (1965). *Priestly Celibacy and Maturity*. New York: Sheed and Ward.

Osborne, Kenan B. (1988). *Priesthood: A History of the Ordained Ministry in the Roman Catholic Church*. New York: Paulist Press.

Perri, William D. (1992). "The Dominant/Submissive, Sociopathic/Histrionic Archetype." Spring, 52, pp. 39-49.

Perri, William D.   (1992).   *A multivariant analysis of psychologically evaluated Roman catholic priests and brothers: Comparisons between diocesan priests, religious priests and religious brothers according to sexual orientation and age*, Unpublished Doctoral Dissertation, Carpinteria, CA: Pacifica Graduate Institute.

Rayburn, Carole A., et. al. (1986). Men, women and religion: Stress within leadership roles. *Journal of Clinical Psychology*, 42 (3), 540-546.

Samuels, Pamela A., and Lester, David. (1985). A preliminary investigation of emotions experienced toward God by Catholic nuns and priests. *Psychological reports*, 56, (3), 706.

Schneider, Kirk J. (1990). *The Paradoxical Self: Toward an Understanding of our Paradoxical Nature*. New York: Plenum Press.

Shrader, Wesley. (1956). Why ministers are breaking down. *Life*, 41, 95-104.

Sinetar, Marsha. (1986). *Ordinary People as Monks and Mystics*. New York: Paulist Press.

Sipe, A.W.R. (1988). Outpatient response to sexual problems of Catholic Religious. *National Guild of Catholic Psychiatrists*, 32, 42-57.

Sipe, A.W. Richard. (1995). *Sex, Priests and Power: Anatomy of a Crisis*. New York: Brunner/Mazel.

Tetlow, Joseph A. (1985). A dialogue on the sexual maturing of celibates. *Studies in the Spirituality of Jesuits*, xvii, 3, 1-34.

Thomas, Gordon. (1986). *Desire and Denial: Celibacy and the Church*. Boston: Little, Brown and Company.

Villiger, John-Baptist. (1983). *The Celibacy of the Priest in the Course of Church History*. Johannesburg, South Africa: Premier Typographers Ltd.

Wallace, Ann M. (1985). Initial encounters of religious and priests with psychotherapy. *Psychotherapy Patient*, 1, (3), 147-158, Special issue: Psychotherapy and the religiously committed patient.

Washa, Robert A. *Dogmatism and its relationship to attitudes toward sexual behavior among Roman Catholic priests of the Diocese of Brooklyn*. Unpublished doctoral dissertation, Adelphi University. (University Microfilms No. DDK78-17483).

Whitlock, G. (1959). The relationship between passivity of personality and personal factors related to the choice of the ministry as a vocation. *Dissertation Abstracts International*, 59, 5029.

Of Related Interest

The Poor Are the Church
A Conversation with Father Joseph Wresinski,
Founder of the Fourth World Movement
Gilles Anouil

Through his conversations with Gilles Anouil, Fr. Wresinski relates what he has learned from the poor, as well as his hopes and fears for the poor and for the Church. He traces the development of the Fourth World Movement, reflects on what it means to give priority to the poorest and challenges readers to see poverty in a profoundly different way, not just as destitution or oppression but as a social isolation created by all of us.
1-58595-183-8; 6 x 9; 208 pp; $16.95 X-25.

Brave New Church
From Turmoil to Trust
William J. Bausch

Father Bill Bausch knows about parish life in the Catholic church firsthand. In this, his latest offering, he focuses on twelve challenges facing the church today. He then considers the transitions and responses that can move the church forward as it seeks to minister to parishioners of the twenty-first century. Father Bausch writes in a clear, informative, and uplifting style and he frames his arguments in a way that is both pastoral and incisive, shaping his ideas and suggestions with solid historical background and strong Catholic principles.
1-58595-135-8, 320 pp, $16.95 (J-85)

Catholic Social Teaching and Movements
Marvin Krier Mich

Putting human faces on the Church's social teachings: that's what this unique book is about. The author aims to tell the story of Catholic social tradition from the perspective of the official teachings and the movements and persons that expressed and shaped that teaching.
0-89622-936-X, 488 pp, $29.95 (J-06)

Available at religious bookstores or from:
TWENTY-THIRD PUBLICATIONS
A Division of Bayard   PO BOX 180 • MYSTIC, CT 06355
1-800-321-0411 • FAX: 1-800-572-0788 • E-MAIL: ttpubs@aol.com
www.twentythirdpublications.com
Call for a free catalog